In a nation full of chui
programs and personalitie
voice calling us back to ˌ˞ˌˢᵉⁿce of the
Lord. *Give No Rest!* urges the American church to learn from King David in his unwavering desire to build a dwelling place for God. Lee has spent years doing just that, implanting prayer and worship into the very heart of the churches he pastors. He instructs other church leaders on how to do the same in this informative and compelling book that is biblical, practical, and inspiring. I highly encourage everyone to read it!

Mike Bickle
International House of Prayer, Kansas City, MO

Lee, put the trumpet to your mouth! Call the Church back to Jesus and His Presence! Spread the message of this book until we're prostrated in tears of holy desperation for God and His glory. May our cities once again be shaken as the lightnings of God flash through the streets. "Unto Him be glory in the Church!"

Bob Sorge
Author, *Secrets of the Secret Place*

This is one of my favorite pastors writing on one of my favorite subjects. The Presence of Jesus is once again becoming priority for the people of God. As God raised up King David to redirect His people back to His Presence, a new breed of leaders are emerging today and doing the same thing. Lee Cummings is uniquely positioned to write on this subject as both a local pastor and a prophetic teacher of our time. *Give No Rest!* is the fruit of a life lived in pursuit of the Presence of Jesus in prayer and worship. There is a massive cultural shift coming to the Church, and this book provides needed language and direction for the hour ahead.

Michael Miller
Lead Pastor, UPPERROOM, Dallas TX

My friend Lee Cummings walks with a unique courage and grace for our generation. Few men have provoked a hunger for God like he has. Lee is a man on fire, and he loves the Church to whom he is writing. May this book ignite a renewed passion to pursue the Presence of God until He comes.

Brian Kim
Pastor, House Denver
Founder, Acts School of Ministry, Denver, CO

GIVE NO REST!

A RENEWED COMMITMENT TO PURSUE GOD'S PRESENCE IN PRAYER AND WORSHIP IN THE AMERICAN CHURCH

LEE CUMMINGS

ISBN: 979-8-9884196-1-7 (paperback)

ISBN: 979-8-9884196-2-4 (e-book)

I dedicate this book to my granddaughter Rees Margot Dillon, who went to be with Jesus after ten days on this earth. Born on Ascension Day and died on Pentecost Sunday, she was named after the great intercessor, Rees Howells.

"We didn't have you here for long, Rees Margot Dillon, but we know we will one day be together longer than we have been apart. Until that day, granddaughter, we will give no rest!"

CONTENTS

FOREWORD

The greatest longing in the heart of God is to fully dwell on the earth with His people. King David is among the rare few in history who touched this longing and gave himself to seeing the fullness of this manifested in his generation.

In *Give No Rest!* Lee Cummings not only brilliantly articulates where we are at prophetically in this hour, but his life is one that is consumed with the same vow that consumed King David many years ago: "I will not enter my house or go into my bed, I will not give sleep to my eyes or slumber to my eyelids, until I find a place for the Lord, a dwelling place for the Mighty One of Jacob" (Psalm 132:3–5).

God is remembering David and his vow not to rest until God rests by marking a new generation of leaders and believers who have a bigger vision than just more money and comfort. This new breed wants to see God's manifest Presence back at the center of His Church.

I cannot overstate how important this book is for the Church in this hour! We must give no rest, Church, until we find a resting place for His Presence.

Corey Russell

Author, *Teach Us to Pray*

ONE

THE VIRUS OF CONSUMER CHRISTIANITY

SOMETHING IS wrong with the American church. When we look at the condition of the American church, especially over the last few years, we have to ask ourselves a question: *What has taken place that has brought us to a crossroads, to this cultural and prophetic moment?*

We can't judge the Church in the West the way we judge the rest of the Church around the globe. When we go to other places around the world—places in Africa, Asia, and South America, for example—the Church looks and functions vastly different. The Church on these continents doesn't necessarily have the wealth, the leadership resources, the development methods, or the church growth models that we have in America. Yet the Church on these continents is thriving. It evidences what we read about in the Acts of the apostles. What the Church in Africa, Asia, and South America has is power. And it's the very thing the American church has little of.

WEAKENED BY CONSUMER CHRISTIANITY

Within this decade, we have been confronted by our powerlessness. More specifically, we've come face-to-face with the weaknesses or even failures of our leaders, our methodologies, and our models. COVID-19 did not cause these things. It only revealed them.

While we were masking up to protect ourselves and others during the pandemic, God unmasked the consumer Christianity infecting the West and infecting the heart and prophetic imagination of His people in the West. *The virus of the American consumer culture infiltrated the heart of the Church like a COVID-19 spike protein latching onto the cell of its host.*

A. W. Tozer (1897–1963), the man some called a twenti-eth-century prophet, wrote about "a generation of Christians reared among push buttons and automatic machines" who applied "machine-age methods" to their "relations with God."[1] And the results, Tozer claimed, "are all about us: shallow lives, hollow religious philosophies, . . . the glorification of men, . . . salesmanship methods, the mistaking of dynamic personality for the power of the Spirit."[2] He said, "These and such as these are the symptoms of an evil disease, a deep and serious malady of the soul."[3] He was talking in his day about our day and the consumer-driven culture harming our souls.

Indeed, consumer Christianity has substituted the Presence for personalities, systems, and paradigms. The American church has used these to attract followers, keep followers, and host events. We have used these to gain wealth and influence.

Don't get me wrong. I'm a pastor. I'm a church planter. And I love the Church of Jesus Christ. The statements I'm making are not meant as a condemnation against the Bride of Christ. I'm merely pointing out that the system and structure adorning the Church in America—the consumer model of Christianity—has been weighed and found wanting.

Consumer Christianity has placed self at its center. The sad truth is the American consumer culture has ransacked our houses of worship and has weakened us as a Church and as a people. And it has weakened our pastors and leaders as well.

According to research conducted by the Barna Group,

Over half of pastors who have considered quitting full-time ministry (56%) say "the immense stress of the job" has factored into their thoughts on leaving. Beyond these general stressors, two in five pastors (43%) say "I feel lonely and isolated," while 38 percent name "current political divisions" as reasons they've considered stepping away.[4]

Stress, isolation, and political divisions are the experience of many within the American church, but that's not all!

In addition to the unmasking of our weaknesses, we've seen the moral failures of high-profile ministries. We've seen the deconstruction movement and the doctrinal demolition of an entire generation of people. Many of these have forsaken the Faith because their theologians have shifted from our ancient Church fathers and history to present-day TikTok clerics and other social media influencers.

Furthermore, we've witnessed and experienced denominational splintering over issues that would cause the prophetic founders of those denominational movements to roar like lions if they were still here. We've also seen the infection in the American church of a political spirit to where we're actually more passionate about politics than we are about God's Presence.

What have all these things produced? *A great polarization within the American church that is revealing our weaknesses and limited power.*

Most of the time, when humanity exposes weakness, it's done to invalidate and shame. When God exposes weakness, especially in His Church, however, He does so to qualify, strengthen, and heal. He does so because of His great mercy, grace, and love. He does so because He has a plan and future in mind for His people, the nations, and the world. And that's good news for us all.

THE ANTIDOTE

What is the antidote to the virus of consumer Christianity? How should we respond to the great polarization? What does God have in store for His Church?

For one thing, we shouldn't walk away from the Church. We shouldn't "wash our hands" of it as if the Church's best days are behind us. Neither should we see the Church as irrelevant in these days or unfit to address society's ever-changing challenges.

Too many have joined in the antiphonal chanting, where one side declares, "I love Jesus," while the other side responds, "But I can't stand His followers." Or "We need to decentralize and get rid of our buildings," says one group while the other says, "We need to build bigger and better." If we don't have Presence, we're just building structures and systems that were meant for God, but now, we have them without Him.

Though I'm grateful for what has happened in 2023 on college campuses like Asbury University and in prayer rooms and churches across this great land, we need more. I want more. I don't know about you, but I'm so ready and so hungry and so desperate for His Presence that, if His Presence isn't going to come, none of this stuff matters.

The right music, the fog machine incense, the hot Insta Reels of services, and the recognizable brand message aren't cutting it. None of these will provide us with an answer. We're just dizzying ourselves, trying to be everything to everybody. We're spun about by every voice. We must stop offering up no solutions as solutions.

If the Church is to regain our equilibrium, we will need a healing in our spiritual ear, and we will need a brand-new order. I believe that's what God's plan is for us.

A NEW ORDER

We need the Presence of God restored back to the center of the Church in the West the way that it has been in previous historic revivals and other reformations. Our man-centered methodology needs to be folded up and put away. Our priesthood and even our systems need to be reconsidered.

For over a year, I have asked God two questions: (1) What is *Your* diagnosis of the American church? (2) What is the remedy? Each time I have asked God these questions, He has brought me back to the life of David. As a matter of fact, David is the prototype of who God wants us to be to our generation. And the biblical narrative of his life provides for us both the diagnosis and the antidote to the sickness infecting the American church.

David isn't the only helpful example to us, however. The very beginnings of the Church as recorded in Acts provide us with what can happen in the American church and in cities across our country if we respond appropriately to the great pressure we're experiencing, living in the context of an increasingly antagonistic and antichrist culture.

I believe God is giving the Church in Western civilization a moment to step back and figure out where we have been and where we need to go. And, if we're honest, we've been struggling to put our finger on exactly what it is that we feel, sense, and know. We don't seem to have words for where we are or why we are here or what we must do to move forward. But it's here at this point, this crossroads, as it were, where God is graciously and mercifully providing us with an opportunity to reorient our bearings and regain our equilibrium.

I believe we are at the same intersection that King David found himself at on one of the most significant moments of his life and leadership. He came to an intersection between Gibeon and Jerusalem, an intersection of destiny. As we will see in the ensuing pages, David took a hard right and set his face toward Zion. But what are *we* going to do? Are we going to go back to Gibeon, the place of Moses' Tabernacle, representing the old system and the old structure?

No, my friend, we are going to take a hard right and say, "At all costs, no matter what it takes, we will have the Presence of God at the center of our lives and at the center of His Church." We must make a hard pivot toward His Presence being more than a prop in our lives and services. His Presence must be an absolute priority that we are desperate to host and honor.

I also believe there are things happening in the heavenly and earthly realms that are coming to another intersection of sorts. This intersection has all the volatility and potential power of spiritual nuclear material. And when the American church begins to respond in prayer and worship, both the Church and our country will begin to experience a book of Acts detonation of Kingdom power and purity of seismic proportions.

God will have centerstage, and His Presence will become our priority once again. Let's renew our commitment to pursue God's Presence in our personal and corporate prayer and worship. Like David of old, we must *give no rest* to our eyes until we have made a resting place for the Presence of our God! It's our only hope and only course— to put all eyes back on the One "who is over all and through all and in all."[5]

---

1. A. W. Tozer, *The Pursuit of God* (Camp Hill, PA: Christian Publications, Inc., 1993), 65.
2. Ibid.
3. Ibid.
4. Leaders & Pastors, "Pastors Share Top Reasons They've Considered Quitting Ministry in the Past Year," The Barna Group, April 27, 2022, https://www.barna.com/research/pastors-quitting-ministry/, accessed April 1, 2023.
5. Ephesians 4:6

TWO

DAVID, THE DISTINCTIVE PRESENCE & ISRAEL

GOD DESCRIBED David as a man after His heart.[1] I don't know of a better epitaph written by God. But how could God say that about a man who took another man's wife and had the other man killed on the front line in battle?[2] A man who failed to discipline his sons?[3] A man who was "incited by Satan" to take a census that led to the deaths of 70,000 Israelites?[4]

God could say it because David loved Him and trusted wholly in His mercy. Overall, David possessed certain qualities that proved irresistible to God. For example, he desired to please God more than people. Acts 13:22 informs us that God said, "I have found in David the son of Jesse a man after my heart, who will do *all my will.*" He would do all God's will because he was committed to God's purpose and desired to please God more than please anyone else in his life. David had a teachable and tender heart. When he failed, he repented.[5] And did I mention David's loyalty? He was a fiercely loyal friend. David was:

- loyal to Saul even when the king attempted to kill him.[6]
- loyal to Jonathan even after Jonathan's death.[7]
- loyal to outcasts who came to him in the wilderness.[8]
- loyal to God in serving God's purpose "in his own generation."[9]

God could say such a man was after His heart more specifically because, *somewhere in David's obscurity and youthful hiddenness, David had become obsessed with giving God what God has always wanted—a dwelling place in the midst of His people, where heaven and earth come together in perfect union again.*

Perhaps David's passionate pursuit of God was best expressed by his son Solomon, who has often been credited with having written:

[David] swore to the Lord and vowed to the Mighty One of Jacob, "I will not enter my house or get into my bed, I will not give sleep to my eyes or slumber to my eyelids, until I find a place for the Lord, a dwelling place for the Mighty One of Jacob."

PSALM 132:2–5

When David expressed this desire of his heart to the prophet Nathan, David said, "Behold, I dwell in a house of cedar, but the ark of the covenant of the Lord is under a tent."[10] To David, finding a "place for the Lord" meant finding a permanent place for the ark of the covenant. That's what the ark meant to him—a dwelling place for God Himself, a place for His Presence.

The ark of the covenant—also known as the ark of the testimony, the ark of God, or the ark of His power—was more than a piece of Tabernacle furniture. Not only was it rich in history and powerful in symbolism, but the ark was central to the covenantal identity of Israel and critical to the physical and spiritual welfare of the nation. To understand how precious the ark was to David and Israel, we must retrace its history.

FOLLOWING THE ARK

We first hear of the ark of the covenant in Exodus 25. It follows on the heels of an incredible event—the ratification of the Mosaic covenant.[11] It was quite a scene. Moses, Aaron, the elders of Israel, and indeed *all* Israel gathered at Mount Sinai. The Book of the Covenant was read, sacrifices were made, and blood was sprinkled on the altar and the people. Then God called Moses, Aaron, Nadab, Abihu, and the seventy elders to come up the mountain but only so far. The people, however, were to remain at the base of Sinai.

What happened next was a precursor to heavenly realities we read about in books like Ezekiel and Revelation:

> Then Moses and Aaron, Nadab, and Abihu, and seventy of the elders of Israel went up, and they saw the God of Israel. There was under his feet as it were a pavement of sapphire stone, like the very heaven for clearness. And he did not lay his hand on the chief men of the people of Israel; they beheld God, and ate and drank.
>
> EXODUS 24:9–11

"They beheld God" and didn't die! In fact, they ate and drank in His Presence. But then Moses was called up further into the cloud that covered the mountain. The glory of God on the mountain "was like a devouring fire . . . in the sight of the people of Israel. Moses entered the cloud and went up on the mountain . . . forty days and forty nights."[12]

What we read next in chapter 25 are God's instructions to Moses regarding the building of the Tabernacle and its furnishings, and the ministry of the priesthood.

First, God told Moses to collect contributions from the people for the building of the Tabernacle. The very next instruction God gave Moses was to build the ark of the covenant of acacia wood and gold along with the mercy seat that was to be placed upon the ark. Then God said to Moses:

There I will meet with you, and from above the mercy seat, from between the two cherubim that are on the ark of the testimony, I will speak with you about all that I will give you in commandment for the people of Israel.

EXODUS 25:22

The ark of the covenant was the place of the Presence. Once built, it would rest in the Most Holy Place behind the veil. The high priest would enter behind the veil once a year on the Day of Atonement, taking the sacrificial blood from the brazen altar and sprinkling the blood on the mercy seat. This atoned for the past sins of the children of Israel, making them clean before the Lord.

When Moses finally came down from the mountain top, he found all Israel worshipping a golden calf they had made. God's anger burned hot against the people.[13] But Moses' intercession prevailed: "And the Lord relented from the disaster that he had spoken of bringing on his people."[14] Still, the people tried to continue in their rebellion, but it was met with God sending them a plague.

The Presence of God was what had distinguished Israel from every other people and nation around them. In Exodus 33:15–16, Moses underscored this when he petitioned God:

If your presence will not go with me, do not bring us up from here. For how shall it be known that I have found favor in your sight, I and your people? Is it not in your going with us, so that we are distinct, I and your people, from every other people on the face of the earth?

This was their covenantal identity, their distinctive as a people. And it continued to be so through the years. Every time the Israelites picked up stakes to follow the pillar of cloud or the pillar of fire, the ark went with them. Set on poles and carried by Levites, the ark moved from place to place this way. When the Israelites camped, the mobile Tabernacle would be erected and the ark of God placed once again in the Most Holy Place behind the veil.

Then during the time of Joshua—when Israel came to the River Jordan to cross into the Promised Land—the ark was carried in front of the people. As the priests' feet stepped into the river, the waters "stood and rose up in a heap very far away," and the people crossed over on dry ground.[15] When the priests came up out of the water, the waters were released to flow once more.[16]

The ark was centerstage in the march around Jericho. The order of the procession was like this: armed men followed by seven priests blowing trumpets, followed by the ark of the covenant carried on its poles by the Levites, followed by a rearguard of armed men. Once a day for six days, they marched in that order. But on the seventh day, the ark went around the city seven times. "By faith" and with a great shout, the Presence brought down the imposing walls of Jericho.[17]

Then someone "broke faith" with the covenant of the Lord and took items from Jericho that had been devoted for destruction. It's interesting that Joshua 7:1 says, "But *the people* of Israel broke faith in regard to the devoted things." One man's breach resulted in Israel's defeat, in the deaths of thirty-six men, and in despair coming over all the people.

In response, Joshua tore his clothes and fell on his face before the ark—the representation of the covenant—until the evening, after which God spoke to him, telling Joshua that someone had kept the "accursed things." Achan confessed to his sin. He was the guilty party, and the judgment was death to him and all his house.[18] He and his family and livestock were stoned to death, their corpses burned. And great stones were heaped over the bodies of Achan and his family. The place was called the Valley of Achor, the Valley of Trouble.

Soon after, we read that Joshua erected an altar at Mount Ebal.

And there, in the presence of the people of Israel, he wrote on the stones a copy of the law of Moses, which he had written. And all Israel, sojourner as well as native born, with their elders and officers and their judges, stood on opposite sides of the ark before the Levitical priests who carried the ark of the covenant of the Lord, half of them in front of Mount Gerizim and half of them in front of Mount Ebal, just as Moses the servant of the

Lord had commanded at the first, to bless the people of Israel. And afterward he read all the words of the law, the blessing and the curse, according to all that is written in the Book of the Law.

JOSHUA 8:32–34

SOMETHING CHANGED

Nonetheless, the Valley of Trouble marked the beginning of a change in Israel's relationship with God and His ark. Though the Israelites continued to conquer city after city and king upon king in their Promised Land, and each tribe received its appropriated inheritance, the people began to go after other gods.

In Judges 2:1–3, right before Joshua died, the angel of the Lord appeared and said to Israel,

I brought you up from Egypt and brought you into the land that I swore to give to your fathers. I said, "I will never break my covenant with you, and you shall make no covenant with the inhabitants of this land; you shall break down their altars." But you have not obeyed my voice. What is this you have done? So now I say, I will not drive them out before you, but they shall become thorns in your sides, and their gods shall be a snare to you.

God had kept His covenant. His ark was still present among them, but things had changed as the people kept mixing their religious practices with those of other nations. The thorns of ungodly cultures pricked their sides, injecting poison. (Sounds familiar, doesn't it?) Israel had become ensnared by other gods, just as God had said. A generation soon passed away, leaving "another generation after them . . . who did not know the Lord or the work which He had done for Israel."[19]

What we are told next in Judges 2:11–23 is the sin cycle of the nation during the time of the judges: Israel did what was evil in God's sight, God allowed their enemies to oppress them, Israel was in great distress, God sent judges to deliver them, and Israel would once again do evil in the sight of God, thus continuing the cycle.

Four times in the book of Judges, we read something like, "In those days there was no king in Israel."[20] And two of those four times these words followed that statement, "Everyone did what was right in his own eyes," as if the presence of a natural king could totally correct that.[21]

The next time we read about the ark in Scripture is in Judges 20:27–28, when the children of Israel asked if they should go up against one of their own tribes—the tribe of Benjamin.

> And the people of Israel inquired of the Lord (for the ark of the covenant of God was there in those days, and Phinehas the son of Eleazar, son of Aaron, ministered

before it in those days), saying, "Shall we go out once more to battle against our brothers, the people of Benjamin, or shall we cease?"

Here's evidence that the ark was no longer centerstage. Its very presence among the people was contained in a parenthetical statement. It was like the writer was saying, "Uh, by the way, the ark of God was there."

Sure, the ark was functional. It could still be used for direction, still good enough to ensure Israel got help to address a problem. However, this statement shows us the God of Abraham, Isaac, and Jacob and the ark the Israelites had held special and sacred had shifted from being, respectively, the distinctive Presence and their identity to merely being useful. *And there is nothing more dangerous than when the hearts of God's people begin to consider His Presence in their midst as useful—the means that justify the ends.*

THE LOST ARK

In 1 Samuel 4, we next hear about the ark during a battle between the Philistines and the Israelites. The Israelites were encamped at Ebenezer and the Philistines at Aphek. A battle ensued that resulted in the deaths of about 4,000 fighting men of Israel.[22] The elders then sent for the ark of the covenant to come to the battlefield from Shiloh (about twenty miles away). Poor 98-year-old Eli, the blind priest, was anxious about the ark's return to Shiloh after the battle, so he waited by the gate, his heart trembling.[23]

Eli's two sons, Hophni and Phinehas, were corrupt priests, yet they attended the ark to the battlefield. When all was said and done after the next battle with the Philistines, 30,000 Israelite fighting men were dead, the ark was captured, and Hophni and Phinehas were killed as well. Then, when news got back to anxiety-ridden Eli, specifically when he heard about the ark, he "fell over backward from his seat by the side of the gate, and his neck was broken and he died, for the man was old and heavy."[24]

The Philistines took the ark to their temple and set it up next to their god, Dagon. "And when the people of Ashdod arose early the next day . . . Dagon had fallen face downward . . . before the ark of the Lord."[25] The Philistines put Dagon back up where he had been, but then the next morning, the god fell down again. This time, "the head of Dagon and both his hands were lying cut off on the threshold. Only the trunk of Dagon was left."[26]

The Presence of God among the Philistines wasn't done yet. God sent tumors and boils upon the people. It was so bad that the Philistines wanted to get rid of the ark because they realized it was the cause for their outbreak. The ark was removed from Ashdod and taken to Gath, and tumors came upon the people there. It was then moved into Akron, but a "deathly panic" went throughout the city so that "the men who did not die were struck with tumors, and the cry of the city went up to heaven."[27]

For seven months, the ark was in Philistine country, and the people were desperate for it to be taken away. No city wanted it! They wanted to send it back to the Israelites, so they put it on a cart with two lowing milk cows yoked to it. And the cows crossed it over the border into Beth Shemesh. The Philistines were like, "Here you go, Israel. You can have your god back because this is not going well."

The ark was taken to the house of Abinadab at Kiriath-jearim. It stayed there for "some twenty years."[28]

Instead of Israel valuing the Presence, they just left the ark at Abinadab's house. They were content having it out of the enemy's hands and in the outskirts of their land. They were okay with the ark being marginalized. Must be they didn't think it was useful to them anymore. Though it had made it across the border and into Israel's territory, the ark wasn't placed back at the center of the culture.

1. See 1 Samuel 13:14 and Acts 13:22.
2. See 2 Samuel 11:4–5, 16–17.
3. See 2 Samuel 13:14–29; 16:15–23.
4. 1 Chronicles 21:1
5. See Psalm 51.
6. See 1 Samuel 24.
7. See 2 Samuel 9.
8. See 1 Samuel 22:1–2.
9. Acts 13:36
10. 1 Chronicles 17:1
11. See Exodus 24.
12. Exodus 24:17–18
13. See Exodus 32:9–10.

14. Exodus 32:14
15. Joshua 3:14–16
16. See Joshua 4:18.
17. Hebrews 11:30
18. See Joshua 7:19–26.
19. Judges 2:10
20. Judges 17:6; 18:1; 19:1; 21:25
21. Judges 17:6; 21:25
22. See 1 Samuel 4:2.
23. See 1 Samuel 4:13.
24. 1 Samuel 4:18
25. 1 Samuel 5:3
26. 1 Samuel 5:4
27. 1 Samuel 5:11–12
28. 1 Samuel 7:2

THREE

THE PRIORITY OF PRESENCE

WITH THE ARK long abandoned at Abinadab's house, the people began to look for another structure or system to establish them further as a nation among nations. The people wanted their own representation and leadership to look like that of the other nations. And Saul fit the bill.

Saul was this larger-than-life, good-looking wealthy guy from the smallest tribe of Israel, a tribe that had experienced some scandal before Saul was born.[1] But that only gave him a little something more to add to his "bad boy" image. He was tall, head and shoulders above everybody else. And he had great hair. From all looks and appearances, he had celebrity, and he was powerful—outwardly powerful, that is. Inwardly, Saul was weak; he even saw himself as "little," which probably had something to do with him being a Benjaminite.[2] Nevertheless, Saul was the man—the king—Israel wanted.

The prophet and judge who would anoint Saul king of Israel was Samuel. As a boy, Samuel had slept in the Tabernacle within safe proximity to the ark of the Presence, but he was now an old man. Samuel's sons were next in line as judges, but they were crooked men who "took bribes and perverted justice."[3] This probably galvanized Israel to demand that God give them a king. They didn't want Samuel's sons to be their leaders. *So, God gave the people what they wanted, a king who was a mere reflection of their own insecurity.* He gave them a king who mirrored their corrupted hearts so that every time they saw King Saul, his actions, his insecurities, and his self-absorption, they were seeing their own reflection of their infected state. They had exchanged Presence for personage, Distinctive for common, Invisible for visible, King for king.

When God ordained Saul as the king of Israel, Samuel took a man-made flask of oil and poured the oil over Saul's head.[4] The very flask is a symbol of the anointing that is in response to the demands of people or consumerism. Although Saul's beginnings as king evidenced the anointing of God, the coming together of the people, and military success, he was rejected by God in the end. He didn't obey God's instructions to destroy all the Amalekites, including their king and animals.[5] It makes you wonder why God chose Saul to be king in the first place. I guess sometimes we are better at seeing our own weaknesses and flaws in the reflection of others than we are at seeing them in the reflection of ourselves in the mirror. In the end, God sent Samuel to anoint another man king.[6]

When Samuel went to the house of Jesse to find the man after God's heart, he went down the line of Jesse's sons, passing over men who "looked the part." It wasn't until he saw the youngest that he heard God say, "Arise, anoint him, for this is he."[7] That was when Samuel poured oil from a horn over David.[8] The horn was made by God, which symbolizes the anointing that comes from God's choice, not man's.

KING DAVID'S PRIORITY

David's rise to power was by no means instantaneous. Many years passed before he took the throne. But during His life in the pasture, he had learned to prioritize God's Presence in his life. And he knew how to pray and worship. We see this throughout the many psalms he wrote. These psalms evidence the many times David had to face enemies and friends, all the while experiencing the faithfulness of God. David braved family rejection, the taunting Goliath, the ever ferocious Philistines, and of course, the jealous Saul. Through all these things, David had fashioned a secret weapon: worship.

According to rabbinic tradition and some scholars, David was the product of an affair, and that explains what David may have meant when he said in Psalm 51:5, "Behold, I was brought forth in iniquity, and in sin did my mother conceive me." Perhaps, if he was a child of an immoral relationship, that could also explain why Jesse didn't have David there in person with his brothers to be presented for selection by the prophet Samuel—why David had to be sent for and retrieved from the pasture somewhere. Whatever may have kept Jesse from initially remembering and presenting David with his brothers, we don't exactly know. But what we do know is David was not his dad's favorite, his brothers chided him when he visited them at the front lines and heard Goliath's mocking, and he was belittled in all their eyes.

However, something happened to David in the pasture with the sheep. He longed to touch the heart of God, and he dug deep into the soil of relationship with God, all the while taking care of the sheep and singing songs to the audience of One. Whether in the pasture or later hiding in caves from the murderous Saul, he searched out the deep emotions of God's heart. So, finally, with all of that behind him, David became king of Israel.

After capturing Jerusalem with all his mighty men around him, he called for all the people and priests to assemble from all the lands of Israel. *And where Saul had neglected God's ark—God's Presence—it became King David's priority.* King David said,

> If it seems good to you and from the Lord our God, let us
> send abroad to our brothers who remain in all the lands
> of Israel, as well as to the priests and Levites in the cities

that have pasturelands, that they may be gathered to us.
Then let us bring again the ark of our God to us, for we
did not seek it in the days of Saul.

1 CHRONICLES 13:2–3

Saul had no use for the ark. Only on one occasion had
he asked for it to be brought back, but even then, he didn't
follow through but rushed on to take matters into his own
hands, as was his custom.[9] David's heart, on the other
hand, was to bring back the ark of the Presence into its
former place of honor and glory.

You can tell a lot about a person with what they do
when they hit their apex of success and wealth, right? I
mean, the guy who only recently got picked up in the draft,
signed with the NFL, and got his signing bonus of
$750,000, what would he go and buy first? A car? A house
for himself? A dream home for his mom and dad? Or does
he go to Disney? I don't know what that guy ends up doing
with his paycheck, but you and I can tell a lot about a
person by what they do first at a high water mark in their
lives.

The word that God had spoken to David many years
ago had now come to fruition: "You shall be shepherd of
my people Israel, and you shall be prince over my people
Israel."[10]

Everybody came together and celebrated him as king.
The wars were behind him, and Israel was unified as he

finally conquered Jerusalem. And his first priority was to say, "Let's go and get the ark of God's Presence. Let's not leave it out in the field somewhere. Let's not leave it at Abinadab's Airbnb. Let's get the ark of the covenant and bring it back!"

David wasn't trying to reestablish a tradition or program of sorts. He wasn't trying to employ some strategy meant to unite the people. Neither was he doing something meant to make him and the tribes happy, as if it was a means to tap into their nostalgic past. No, his priority was rooted in bringing back the Presence of God to the center of Israel as its cultural focus and identity. They would have the power of God among them once more.

---

1. See 1 Samuel 9:1–2 and Judges 19–21.
2. 1 Samuel 15:17
3. 1 Samuel 8:3
4. See 1 Samuel 10:1.
5. See 1 Samuel 15:1–10.
6. See 1 Samuel 16:1–5.
7. 1 Samuel 16:12
8. See 1 Samuel 16:13. King Solomon would later be anointed by Zadok the priest, who "took the horn of oil from the tent and anointed Solomon" (1 Kings 1:39).
9. See 1 Samuel 14:18–19.
10. 1 Chronicles 11:2

FOUR

THE FIRST ATTEMPT TO RECAPTURE THE ARK

ISRAEL WAS ECSTATIC! Gathering at Hebron were people from every tribe of the nation. Let's picture the scene for a moment.

The "men of war" were "arrayed in battle order," and they had come "with a whole heart to make David king over all Israel."[1] The people, too, were "of a single mind to make David king," and "for three days," they were partying it up—"eating and drinking."[2] There was cake and food carried on donkeys and wine and oil and joy as David declared his desire to bring the ark back to Jerusalem.

Can you imagine the singleness of purpose pulsing in the crowd of people? The sense of nationalism and pride? The brotherly love among distant relatives?

It was no wonder that the people agreed to do what their king had asked of them. After all, they were there to celebrate him and their nation, and offer their affirmation of and allegiance to him, their new sovereign. It was within this context that we're told

> David arose and went with all the people who were with him . . . to bring up from there the ark of God, which is called by the name of the Lord of hosts who sits enthroned on the cherubim.
>
> 2 SAMUEL 6:2

And for this special occasion, it would only be right for them to use something that hadn't been used before.

A NEW CART

Second Samuel 6:3 tells us the ark was taken out of Abinadab's house and carried on a new cart. Uzzah and Ahio, Abinadab's sons, became part of the procession as they drove the cart, with Ahio out front. "David and all the house of Israel were celebrating before the Lord, with songs and lyres and harps and tambourines and castanets and cymbals."[3] I mean, it was a great parade—probably the best parade Israel had ever seen, next to the Red Sea crossing after-party, that is. Then something happened that would stop the celebration cold.

> And when they came to the threshing floor of Nacon, Uzzah put out his hand to the ark of God and took hold

of it, for the oxen stumbled. And the anger of the Lord was kindled against Uzzah, and God struck him down there because of his error, and he died there beside the ark of God.

2 SAMUEL 6:6–7

King David's first attempt to bring the ark back front-and-center did not go as planned. Saying it didn't go well is the understatement of understatements. There they were, all trying to usher in the Presence to Jerusalem, when the oxen stumbled, the ark slipped, and Uzzah tried to assist but was struck down dead on the spot!

What did poor Uzzah do to get killed by God? He was only trying to stabilize the ark on the cart after going over some Michigan-sized pothole, wasn't he? From first reading, you have to think Uzzah got a bum rap. He was only trying to help keep the parade going and get the ark to its destination. The problem was the ark was meant to be carried on poles and on the shoulders of priests. God would not be handled.

During Israel's sojourn in the wilderness, God had given them very clear and specific instructions about how the ark was supposed to be transported and carried. *The new cart was man's methodology.* It was how the Philistines had transported the ark when they sent it back over the border. It's how things get moved easily, with the least amount of work or effort by men, but it is not God's method.

God doesn't anoint methods. As E. M. Bounds (1835–1913) said, "The Holy Ghost does not flow through methods, but through men. He does not come on machinery, but on men. He does not anoint plans, but men."[4] God anoints men and women, not strategies.

Poles on the shoulders of those who had been consecrated as priests for such a purpose was God's way. Obviously, David and the sons of Abinadab didn't do it right.

The triumphant return of the Presence went badly, and the place where Uzzah died became known as Perez-uzzah, the place where God broke out against Uzzah.

A WRONG MOVE

Can you imagine trying to do the right thing—trying to honor God in a great way—and someone right there with you dies? Someone who is helping you honor God? Someone God kills for helping? How would you feel? How would you respond?

Well, David was angry *and* afraid. He was angry because of what God did, yet he was afraid of God because of what God did.[5] Wouldn't you be? I know I would.

And David was stuck. He didn't see a way forward. He ended up taking the ark aside to the house of Obed-edom and leaving it there. Obed-edom wasn't even a covenantal member of the house of Israel, but he took in the ark of the covenant, nonetheless, for three months.[6]

I wonder what was going on in David's heart during those three months. More than likely, he was frustrated, and maybe he was even angry still. I imagine him saying, "God, I don't know why You're doing this to me. Here I am trying to do the right thing. I'm trying to bring Israel, this people You've asked me to shepherd, back into a place of covenant faithfulness. I've done everything I know to do. I'm having meetings with people and trying to convince them that this is the right thing to do. And then, when I finally get everybody on board and we go and do it, You show up like this!"

I just see David pacing around in his palace, and to put a modern spin on it, I see him scroll through Instagram. I see him watching these reels from Obed-edom, where Obed-edom says things like, "Man, I just found $15,000 in my bank account. I don't know where it came from or how it got there. . . . I just got a letter from the IRS that said I paid way too much in taxes the last decade, so the IRS is going to pay off my mortgage. . . . My son who can play basketball but was benched because of his height suddenly grew six inches over the last three months, and now he's a starting forward. . . . My marriage is better than ever. It's all good—great even!"

After watching highlight reel after highlight reel, David wants to know what's going on down at Obed-edom's house. So, he slides up into Obed-edom's DM and says, "Hey, what's going on, Obed-edom?"

"It's the ark! It's the Presence of the Lord, King David. God is in my house. I wake up every morning, and He is here. My devotions have gone to a whole new level. I'm reading the Bible, and revelation is blowing up the pages! I'm blessed, sir! Yes, I'm blessed!"

That's it! It pushes David to say, "Let's try again! This time, we'll be meticulous in *how* we do it. We will bring back the ark from Obed-edom's house."

---

1. 1 Chronicles 12:38
2. 1 Chronicles 12:38–39
3. 2 Samuel 6:5
4. E. M. Bounds, *Power through Prayer,* Christian Classics Ethereal Library, https://ccel.org/ccel/bounds/power/power.I_1.html/, accessed April 13, 2023.
5. See 1 Chronicles 13:11–12.
6. See 1 Chronicles 13:14.

FIVE

THE ARK'S RETURN

DAVID BUILT himself a house in his city. And we're told "he prepared a place for the ark of God and pitched a tent for it."[1] In other words, David prepared an environment for God to be honored perpetually by him and all Israel. And that meant that they were going to do things the right way this time. So, David informed the people that only the Levites could carry the ark because "the Lord had chosen them to carry the ark of the Lord and to minister to him forever."[2] This time, King David took extreme measures to carry the ark so that God would be pleased and obeyed. He called all the sons of Aaron and the Levites to consecrate themselves in preparation to bring the ark of God to the place the king had erected for it.[3]

As if that weren't enough, "David also commanded the chiefs of the Levites to appoint their brothers as the singers who should play loudly on musical instruments, on harps and lyres and cymbals, to raise sounds of joy."[4] But there was yet another thing that happened en route: Sacrifices were offered to the Lord. Nothing would be overlooked this time—David made sure of that.

THE BLOODY PARADE

With the Levites carrying the ark with poles on their shoulders and the boisterous singers and musicians in tow, the parade was ready.

> So David and the elders of Israel and the commanders of thousands went to bring up the ark of the covenant of the Lord from the house of Obed-edom with rejoicing. And because God helped the Levites who were carrying the ark of the covenant of the Lord, they sacrificed seven bulls and seven rams. David was clothed with a robe of fine linen, as also were all the Levites who were carrying the ark, and the singers and Chenaniah the leader of the music of the singers. And David wore a linen ephod. So all Israel brought up the ark of the covenant of the Lord with shouting, to the sound of the horn, trumpets, and cymbals, and made loud music on harps and lyres.
>
> 1 CHRONICLES 15:25–28

Once again, the parade throng was on the move. Second Samuel 6 adds something more to help us understand what was happening on this trip back with the ark: "And when those who bore the ark of the Lord had gone six steps, he sacrificed an ox and a fattened animal."[5] Remember there were seven bulls and seven rams sacrificed. So it was one, two, three, four, five, six steps, stop. An animal was then sacrificed. Do you know how hard it was to cut up a bull or even a goat in a sacrificially kosher way? David did it over the course of several miles with rejoicing and musicians and praise. He did it wearing an ephod that was reserved for the priests. David led the way instead of following because David recognized that there was only one King in this procession, and it wasn't him.

Six steps, six is the number in the Bible that typically refers to man. Think of it as David coming to the number of man—the sixth step—and reminding the crowd with him it's all about the blood that cleanses. It's the blood that makes atonement for sin. It's the blood that speaks of covenant with God.

"Six steps, let's do it again. Six steps, let's do it again. Six steps, let's do it again!" It had to have been a bloody parade!

THE INTERSECTION

As they were returning from where the ark had been at Obed-edom's house, David came to an intersection. He could either go left, or he could go right. If he went left, he would take the ark back to the Tabernacle of Moses that was in Gibeon. It was only a couple of miles away. If he went right, however, he would be taking the ark of the Presence to Jerusalem, to the tent which he had pitched for it.

Just imagine the scene for a moment. The musicians were playing. David was out front dancing before the entourage of Levites, singers, musicians, and people. They had traveled several miles with the priests carrying the ark —the Presence of God—on their shoulders. They were all being very, very careful and intentional in everything they were doing. It was here David had to determine where to take the ark for its resting place.

Should I take the ark back to the Tabernacle of Moses and place it in the Holy of Holies, to the way it was laid out in the book of Exodus? That was what everybody expected him to do, but when he arrived at that intersection, David took a hard right because the right turn would lead him directly into the city of Jerusalem—to Mount Zion—where his own palace was. It would take the ark to the tent David had pitched for the Presence. And that was what David did. The king took that sharp right turn.

I am almost positive, when David made that turn, somebody started saying, "King David, we're going the wrong way! This isn't right. We're not headed toward the Tabernacle!"

David was probably so busy dancing and singing that he motioned with his hands in response, trying to wave the person off in an attempt to communicate they were, in fact, headed in the right direction. That might not have sat extremely well with everyone, especially since God struck down Uzzah on the first attempt. They may have been talking among themselves and saying, "What in the world is going on? Somebody's going to die again! We're doing this wrong. We can't go to Jerusalem when the Tabernacle is in Gibeon."

I believe everything shook the moment David turned toward Jerusalem because what David was saying by making that turn was, "God, I'm not content to put You back in the Tabernacle in Gibeon. I don't want things to be the way they were. I want You near me. I want You at the center. I don't want my throne on Zion. I want Your throne on Zion."

David led the parade into Jerusalem—to Mount Zion—where the city of David was. He worshipped God all the way home, and David worshipped God extravagantly. Second Samuel 6:14–15 (NLT) says:

And David danced before the Lord with all his might, wearing a priestly garment. So David and all the people of Israel brought up the Ark of the Lord with shouts of joy and blowing of rams' horns.

Upon his arrival, Michal, his disapproving wife, came out to see him and "said in disgust, 'How distinguished the king of Israel looked today, shamelessly exposing himself to the servant girls like any vulgar person might do!'"[6] I love what his response to her was! It's epic. He said,

I was dancing before the Lord, who chose me above your father and all his family! He appointed me as the leader of Israel, the people of the Lord, so I celebrate before the Lord. Yes, and I am willing to look even more foolish than this, even to be humiliated in my own eyes! But those servant girls you mentioned will indeed think I am distinguished!"

2 SAMUEL 6:21–22 NLT

Talk about a royal smackdown! Nothing or no one was going to deter him from giving God what God wanted— true worship, "in spirit and truth" worship.[7]

The king continued his journey to the exact spot he had prepared for the ark of the Presence. David placed it in the tent he had erected on his property, right next to his own home.

With this act, King David was changing up the order of things. Charles Haddon Spurgeon (1834–1892), the "Prince of Preachers," put it this way:

At that time, in all David's land, there was no proper place for that ark where on the Lord placed the mercy-seat, where prayer could be offered, and where the manifested glory shone forth. All things had fallen into decay, and the outward forms of public worship were too much disregarded; hence the king resolves to be first and foremost in establishing a better order of things.[8]

"Hey, fellas, this is where I want the Presence. I want it right here at my home." With that, the king placed the ark of the Presence in what became known as the tabernacle of David.

---

1. I Chronicles 15:1
2. I Chronicles 15:2
3. See I Chronicles 15:4–14.
4. I Chronicles 15:16
5. 2 Samuel 6:13
6. 2 Samuel 6:20 NLT
7. John 4:23–24
8. C. H. Spurgeon, *The Treasury of David,* vol. III, (Peabody, MA: Hendrickson Publishers, 1988), 146.

SIX

DAVID'S TENT & THE NEW ORDER

PLACING the ark under the tent in Jerusalem was a huge step toward fulfilling the vow King David had made—the vow his son Solomon wrote about in Psalm 132.

> I will not enter my house or get into my bed, I will not give sleep to my eyes or slumber to my eyelids, until I find a place for the Lord, a dwelling place for the Mighty One of Jacob.
>
> PSALM 132:3–5

Though, in the end, King David was not allowed to build a more permanent dwelling for God's Presence—God having designated David's son Solomon to build the Temple—David succeeded in developing the new priestly order of worship that he implemented and ensured

Solomon would continue. And David would later provide Solomon with the very plans for the building of all things related to the Temple.[1]

Looking back at David's history with God, specifically when he was hidden in the back forty of Bethlehem, we recognize he had developed a deep, intimate relationship with the Lord. That relationship went beyond David's position as a shepherd and beyond the expectations of his family as the one left in the pasture. Something rose up in David as a worshipping warrior that made him make that vow to find a dwelling place for God.

David had developed such intimacy with the Lord in the pasture that, when his apex moment of success came, the priority of his life was not about marketing his reign in an opulent or luxurious way. Neither did he go about expanding his territory. Rather, he wanted to put the Presence of God at the center of everything—even next to his own home.

Often, I've read about David and thought, *Why did God allow David to do this? After all, he really was breaking the protocol that God had given of how and where His Presence must be housed and approached.* I believe it had everything to do with a revelation that God had given to David while David was living in obscurity and hiddenness, and I believe the revelation was this: *One day, every believer will be a king and priest before God, will bear the Presence of God, will know God intimately, and will have the Spirit of God abiding within.* It was as if David traveled in time by revelation to understand, not just the law of God, but the heart of God. I believe this revelation is what caused David to know which way to turn when he was at the intersection, choosing Mount Zion over Gibeon.

David chose the place God had chosen:

> For the Lord has chosen Zion; he has desired it for his dwelling place: "This is my resting place forever; here I will dwell, for I have desired it. . . . Her priests I will clothe with salvation, and her saints will shout for joy."
>
> PSALM 132:13–16

David did the intimate thing. He took God with him, as it were, enthroning God at the center of Israel's entire culture and identity. What's interesting about this is, for the next forty years, there were two tabernacles that were coexisting in Israel at exactly the same time. There was the Tabernacle of Moses, and then there was David's tent.

TWO TABERNACLES

The Tabernacle of Moses had three compartments: the outer court, the Holy Place, and the Most Holy Place. It also had its system of sacrifices on the altar, its priesthood, and its ceremony. The Tabernacle of Moses was happening around the clock—24/7. But there was no Presence in that tabernacle.

Now, the other tabernacle, the tent of David in Jerusalem, wasn't compartmentalized. It was wide open. King David appointed some 4,000 Levites. He changed the priesthood so that the Levites ministered to the Lord in song and in prayer.

Then he appointed some of the Levites as ministers before the ark of the Lord, to invoke, to thank, and to praise the Lord, the God of Israel. Asaph was the chief, and second to him were Zechariah, Jeiel, Shemiramoth, Jehiel, Mattithiah, Eliab, Benaiah, Obed-edom, and Jeiel, who were to play harps and lyres; Asaph was to sound the cymbals, and Benaiah and Jahaziel the priests were to blow trumpets regularly before the ark of the covenant of God. Then on that day David first appointed that thanksgiving be sung to the Lord by Asaph and his brothers. . . . So David left Asaph and his brothers there before the ark of the covenant of the Lord to minister regularly before the ark as each day required, and also Obed-edom and his sixty-eight brothers, while Obed-edom, the son of Jeduthun, and Hosah were to be gatekeepers. And he left Zadok the priest and his brothers the priests before the tabernacle of the Lord in the high place that was at Gibeon to offer burnt offerings to the Lord on the altar of burnt offering regularly morning and evening, to do all that is written in the Law of the Lord that he commanded Israel. . . . Heman and Jeduthun had trumpets and cymbals for the music and instruments for sacred song.

1 CHRONICLES 16:4–7, 37–42

Obed-edom was honored to get in on the new priestly worship movement. How about that! But there were singers and musicians all ministering to the Lord before the ark under the pitched tent. The ark was not resting inside the Tabernacle of Moses but under the tabernacle of David. And the Presence of God was there in a tangible, manifested way. Many of the psalms that we have in our Bibles were songs that were prophesied or prayed in David's tabernacle and were recorded by God for proceeding generations—for all of us—to grow and learn from.

For a period of time, then, there were these two tabernacles. Two types of "worship" or "ministry" were going on while only one tabernacle of the two actually had the manifest Presence of God. Moses' Tabernacle had a structure, a priesthood, and a system all without the Presence. It had history and tradition. David's tabernacle had the new order, the new wineskin. It had a new priesthood built around the Presence.

If you were to look topographically at where the ark of the covenant was—under the tabernacle of David—one of the main highways traversed in those days would be within eyesight. People traveled from Egypt, Asia, Babylon, and Persia along a ridge. It was one of the most traveled highways in all of the world—one of the most ancient roads. Thousands of people traveled it as it was a trade route. Every single day, people from Egypt, Arabia, Persia, and Babylon traveled on this trade route and would hear the song of the Lord coming out from under the tent as they passed by. They had to wonder what was going on in Jerusalem. I believe that's what David meant in Psalm 40:3 when he said, "Many will see and fear, and put their trust in the Lord." The travelers along the trade route got to see and hear, so what was going on in prayer and worship from under David's tabernacle was evangelistic in nature.

I can't wrap my mind around what could have motivated anyone in that time to want to hang out at the Tabernacle of Moses. How could anyone go through the motions at Moses' Tabernacle while hearing and seeing the Presence of God in such a powerful and tangible way in David's tabernacle? Yet sacrifices and lighting the candelabra and replacing the table showbread and offering the sacrifices and cleansing out the laver and burning incense to go into a room where there was no Presence were part of the old Tabernacle system. If I were a priest at Gibeon, I would have asked for some PTO and taken a trip to Jerusalem because that was where the Presence was felt and dealt.

GOING THROUGH THE MOTIONS

I'm reminded of a story I heard my friend Rick Renner share. He pastors in Moscow and told me that, years ago when the wall first collapsed allowing him and his family to go into Russia, everything was opening up. They were able to plant one of the first churches in Riga, Latvia. Rick discovered while there that the people had been held under the influence of communism for so long that they did not think as individuals. They thought corporately or collectively. He had an experience that underscored just how much that influence had affected them.

Rick went into a shoe factory where he was given a tour, and only half of the factory was functioning. Rick asked why only half of the factory was active. And this is what he was told in response.

"That half of the factory is where we make right shoes."

"Well," Rick thought for a moment, "what do you do on this half?"

"They are working on the left shoes."

"Why are they working over here and not over there?"

"Because that machine is broken."

"So, all you're making are left shoes?" Rick asked.

"Yes."

"And how long have you been doing this?"

"Four months."

Rick was amazed. He couldn't believe what he was hearing. This factory had only been producing left shoes for months! "Why are you only making left shoes if you don't have the capacity to make the matching shoes?"

"Because that's the way we've always done it."

These workers were going through the motions collectively. You and I know what they were doing didn't make any sense. Who wants to walk around in two left shoes? Who has two left feet, literally, I mean? But the workers had grown used to doing the same old thing the same old way —together. No one spoke up and bucked the system.

Vance Havner (1901–1986), the "most quoted preacher in America," said this: "The devil is not fighting religion. He's too smart for that. He is producing a counterfeit Christianity, so much like the real one that good Christians are afraid to speak out against it."[2]

The American church can have methodologies. We can have structures. We can even have ministries and ordination and clergy. But if we don't have the Presence, we're just building religious structures and systems that are counterfeit Christianity. And if we don't have a praying, worshipping, God-following priesthood, we won't have Presence.

---

1. See 1 Chronicles 28.
2. Vance Havner. AZQuotes.com, Wind and Fly LTD, 2023. https://www.azquotes.com/quote/1184789/, accessed March 10, 2023.

SEVEN

THE DREAM

IN JUNE OF 2020, only a few months into the pandemic, we all were trying to adjust or adapt to the news, the restrictions, and the deaths. Then riots broke out in response to the wrongful death of George Floyd by a police officer. On top of that, we were in the middle of a very turbulent election. Grave injustice, cities set ablaze, global pandemic, financial crisis, and political unrest—America was reeling.

I remember it all sent me to my knees. I asked God, "What is happening? What's all this about? Is this the end of Western civilization because it feels like the barbarians are at the gates—like all our foundations are getting turned upside down?"

I had no immediate answer from Him, only the assurance that He was on the throne and He would take care of me, His Church, and all of it.

June 7, 2020, the Lord awakened me in the middle of the night and gave me a very vivid dream. It was what I like to call a God-voice dream. I remember being lucid and remember very clearly what the Lord spoke to me.

God showed me a lot of things. He showed me a storm gathering in the Church. Leaders in a meeting at a conference were trying to figure out how to respond to the storm, but I heard the voice of the Lord speak in the midst of that dream, and here is what He said, *"Seven days of testing are appointed for the American church—seven days that will define it. These are the days of urgency. There will be praise in the streets of America,"* He continued, *"if there will finally be prayer in My Church in America."*

A TIME OF DIVINE TRANSITION

I woke up, shaking from the inside out, and I journaled the entire dream, word, and experience. I tried, of course, to wrap my head around what the seven days mean. You know, the Bible uses this methodology of a heptad, a week or seven days. I wondered if the seven days represented seven things—actually seven days, seven month, seven years? The Lord soon showed me the seven days represent a period of testing. The seven days don't necessarily represent a specific number of days, weeks, months, or years. They do represent a "week of divine transition." Though that week may be a certain number of years, it's not mine to know. I leave that in God's hands.

But I do know it's a time of divine transition when we will find ourselves in a time of frustration. So, make no mistake about it. We are living in a destiny moment, a transition moment, a crossroads moment, where God is looking at the Church and He is saying, "How are you going to respond in this hour of trying to figure out what to do? How is My Church going to respond in this hour when you're looking at the protests, you're looking at the fires and continued ravaging of cities like Atlanta, Minneapolis, New York, Portland, Seattle, and all the different cities around the world? Do you really want to see praise in the streets instead of protesting in the streets? It's not going to be dependent on what happens in Washington, D. C. It's going to depend upon what happens among the *ecclesia,* the Church of Jesus Christ. If the Church will pray, there will be revival in America."

Church, if we will pray, God will move powerfully. He will restore the Presence, the ark of God, back to the center of the people of God, but He is looking at us and asking us in the time of divine transition, "What are you going to do?"

First Peter 4:17, you know it well, says, "For it is time for judgment to begin at the household of God; and if it begins with us, what will be the outcome for those who do not obey the gospel of God?" When God brings judgment, He always starts with the Church. And God's judgment in the Church is always centered on preparation and discipline. It's course correction. His judgment in His house and among His people is not sent to destroy or to dismantle, but it is sent to discipline and correct and purify. Ultimately, when God brings judgment into the world, it is centered around what the world has done with Jesus in the gospel. But *when God brings judgment into the Church, it's about what we've done with His Presence.*

I believe this period of time that we are in is the divine intersection David faced. Are we going to return to Gibeon and say, "Well, I'm glad the pandemic is over. I'm glad I don't have to wear a mask when I get on an airplane. I'm glad that we can put all that behind us. I'm glad we can get back to church as usual. We can start to employ our strategies and methodologies. We can begin to implement outreaches the way we used to without fear of spreading the virus"?

No! That's not our answer. If you are a church leader and have any of those three-ring binders chock full of church strategies and the like, come close. I want to give you a strong encouragement. Throw them out! Throw out all of your three-ring binders that you have from church growth conferences. Just go ahead and burn them because the priesthood is changing! The order is changing! The new wineskin that God wants to bring is going to emerge, and it is the only thing fit to hold or fit to carry the new wine He is about to outpour.

THE PICTURES

When we started this book, I told you I had been going to God with questions, and each time He took me to the life of His servant David. And I believe what God has shown me for the American church is that it is going to be a purified, praying, and worshipping church. In fact, the Lord gave me a picture of what He is wanting to do in this new order or wineskin, and I drew it in my journal. I have it here for you below:

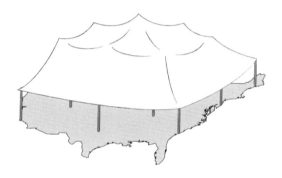

God is raising a tabernacle of David across America.

God gave me this picture, this vision, over America. He wants His Church in America to be stewards of His Presence to impact the culture of our nation. We need to see ourselves as missionaries to the fourth largest mission field on the globe, which is North America. We can no longer afford to see ourselves as Christian America that sends missionaries to other nations. No, *you've been sent here as a prophetic voice to your culture, and here is the thing: You can't be a prophet to your culture if you're a product of your culture. You can't disciple kingdoms if you're being discipled by kingdoms.* So, we must see our country differently.

Here's another picture of what I believe God wants to do in us. He is setting up tent poles across North America.

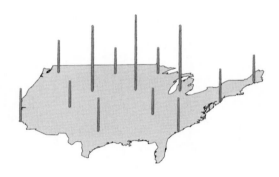

God is raising up tent poles in cities across America.

God showed me North America with tent poles rising up all over the United States in places like Kalamazoo, New York City, Kansas City, and many other cities across the map.

Over the last several years, God has been at work, dismantling the old order while beginning to stir the hearts of leaders to a new order of priesthood. These leaders, like David of old, have been hidden in obscurity and have begun to build churches that will serve as tent poles across North America. These tent poles will serve to hold up the tent covering, housing the Presence and glory of God.

After this season of testing—this divine transition—where we are in this prophetic moment, if we respond correctly, here is what God has in store for our country: God is going to pitch, in the Spirit, the tabernacle of David over North America, where for the first time in a generation we will see the Church in America dominated by the priority of His Presence. *The churches will be praying and worshipping churches whose leaders have made the decision to bring the ark back—and not to the back room or the old order—but to the main stage, to the forefront of everything they do.*

This great polarization I mentioned in chapter one is actually a set-up for a new reformation that is taking place. Recently, someone asked me what I thought God was doing in the Church, and I said, "It depends on which Church you are talking about because if you're talking about the Church in Africa, well, it's a wildfire, baby! If you're talking about the Church in Latin America, it's experiencing full-on revival. If you're talking about the Church in Iran, it's multiplying, and people are giving up their faith in Islam and being martyred. Men in white robes are appearing to people, and angels are giving visions or transcribing the book of John to tailors who are sitting in their shops. It's crazy stuff in Iran. And then if you're talking about the

Church in China, it is exponentially exploding. There is power and Presence in these countries. But if you're talking about America," I said, "or the Church in the West, we're seeing a great polarization that will take place unto a new reformation."

EIGHT

THE ORDER OF DAVID

IN THESE DAYS of divine transition, the Church will experience a reformation, a new order. Like the time of David, I believe we are living in a *kairos* moment in which God is raising up and appointing a new order and priestly anointing. And that new order is what I call the *order of David.*

The order of David is bringing back the Presence to the center of Christian life, Christian activity, and Christian prayer and worship. To do this, God is going to need David-hearted leaders whom He has prepared in the obscurity of the wilderness. Like David, these leaders will give no rest to their eyes until they find a resting place for God. And this will result in an overall change to the priesthood of the Church. I want to describe for you what this order of David will look like.

WHAT IT LOOKS LIKE

First of all, the new order will have leaders who will demon-strate, and not simply delegate, the ministry of prayer. If prayer is one of a hundred ministries of your church, then prayer is not at the center. Speaking to senior church leaders, if you're not passionate about prayer—if you're not leading or demonstrating it—prayer will never take root in your church. It will always be a ministry but never become culture.

Leaders, you've got to lead prayer. You cannot pass it on as merely one of the ministries you tag someone else to oversee. Prayer must be burning in your heart. Get before God and relight the first-love flame again by developing the discipline of prayer in your life and then lead your church in prayer.

The hardest thing we do as pastors is not Sunday mornings. It's prayer meetings. Leading a prayer meeting is like rolling a boulder up a hill. As soon as you take your hand off, the boulder rolls back down.

Lead, model, demonstrate, and talk about prayer. That's what you want to do. You don't want to do a solo prayer series once a year. No, you want to live a life of prayer—a life that demonstrates you're a man or woman of prayer—a leader who prays with and before God's people.

At the formation of the early church, the Twelve made a decision to "devote" themselves "to prayer and to the ministry of the word."[1] Pastor, let me just take a burden off you. You don't have to be the psychologist, the marketing expert, the janitor, the CEO, or the accountant. You just need to devote yourself to the ministry of prayer and the Word. Your first ministry is to God.

When I was a teenager and felt the call of God on my life, the Lord told me way back then, "Your first ministry is to Me, and it will always be to Me." You see, even when I go back into my prayer closet each morning or when I lead prayer in our prayer room at Radiant Church, do you know what Jesus reminds me about? He says, "Everybody else may think of you as Pastor Lee or think of you as a teacher, but you're still that twelve-year-old kid to Me. I love it when you get alone with Me and pray with holy desperation like that twelve-year-old kid."

Second, the new order of David will have churches that will host God's Presence and not handle it. Uzzah got in trouble because he tried to handle the Presence. When you handle something, you control it. *The Presence of God is not something we control or manipulate.*

Now, there is a difference between handling God's Presence and hosting it. We don't want the Presence because it's useful to us. Remember the children of Israel were guilty of that. Neither do we attempt to manipulate it or God's people. We want to revere God, and we want to honor and host His Presence so that He is exalted and glorified among us, and He is worshipped as holy because He is holy. To this, we give Him room to move. We provide Him space and time, showing Him that we mean it when we say, "Lord, have Your way. Do what You want to do among us." We also honor Him with our praise and worship and giving.

Third, the order of David will bring prayer from the back room to centerstage of the Church. Prayer must happen where all the people are gathered. It must be demonstrated and taught front-and-center in our worship services and gatherings. In *Preacher and Prayer*, E. M. Bounds wrote:

> The pulpit of this day is weak in praying. The pride of learning is against the dependent humility of prayer. Prayer is with the pulpit too often official—a performance for the routine of service. Prayer is not to the modern pulpit the mighty force it was in Paul's life or Paul's ministry. Every preacher who does not make prayer a mighty factor in his own life and ministry is weak as a factor in God's work and is powerless to project God's cause on this world.[2]

I've even heard about movements that discourage people from leading in intercessory prayer from the platform on Sunday mornings. Leaders in such movements actually tell worship leaders and pastoral staff not to make room for intercessory moments in their Sunday morning worship services.

That's so sad because people are hungry for the Presence of God. They are desperate for an encounter with God. Our churches will never compete with Disney and its technology. But we have something that nothing in this world's system can compete with—it's the real, tangible, manifest Presence of Almighty God in our midst. Lean into your strength, pastors. Pray and welcome His Presence. Lead God's people in an intercessory moment because God is going to develop churches that bring prayer centerstage.

Fourth, God is looking for worship leaders who will move from a "seeker mentality" to a "seek Him orientation." We don't want to approach worship as if it's something that's *for* us— as if it's something we enjoy because of what we get out of it. Worship is not about us. *Worship is about God. We worship Him.* We don't sing songs to hear ourselves sing or to jam for our own pleasure.

Worship isn't about the seeker. It's not meant to impress the seeker. It's not about the playlist. It's not consumer driven. We need worship where God is centerstage. We need worship leaders whose entire orientation is to seek the Lord and honor Him with heart, soul, mind, and strength.

Fifth, God is looking for His Church to shift from a celebrity culture to a surrendered culture. In the Davidic order, it's all about having hearts surrendered to the Lord, hearts humbled before the Lord, hearts worshipping the Lord. The celebrity culture is a whitewashed culture. It's all outward appearance with flash and sparkle rather than an inward posture of a humble heart.

Sixth, the order of David will have a people who reject the political spirit in order to embrace a prophetic mantle. Church, we're called to be a prophetic voice, not a political echo.

And make no mistake about it, the political spirit wants to neuter the Church of Jesus by offering us a quick-fix bowl of lentils. In our frustration at where culture is going, it offers us an easily made bowl of lentils that will satisfy by us getting angry and jumping into the rhetoric that is being echoed on every news network in the 24-hour news cycle. But it takes the heart of a man or a woman who has encountered the Lord to forgo the lentils so that they don't lose their birthright to be a prophetic voice with a higher mandate.

Seventh, the new order will have a generation of leaders consumed with a vow rather than the approval of men. There is a verse that the Lord has had me camping out in. I've memorized it as it is pertinent for the days in which we are living. It's Galatians 1:10, where Paul said, "For am I now seeking the approval of man, or of God? Or am I trying to please man? If I were still trying to please man, I would not be a servant of Christ."

We all want to be liked. We all want to grow. We all want to reach people for Christ. We all want to see people's lives changed. I understand that we often think there must be an exchange in the transaction for reaching and impacting people for Christ. We can feel as if we need to do certain things for people—like provide them a place at the table, so to speak, so that they feel welcome and comfortable. But if we're not careful, we can move into doing things to please people instead of doing things that please God. "I don't want to lose my voice to this demographic of people," we might say. And that starts to influence our behavior. We bend over backward not to say or do anything to offend the demographic because we want them to feel "at home" or comfortable in our churches. But how often do we try to please our guests so they will continue to come to our church only not to see those guests return?

In the early days of ministry, my wife, Jane, and I had this joke. Anytime a church guest told us, "This is it! This is our church!" We would look at each other, and one of us would say, "Well, we'll never see them again. Bye. It was great to meet them anyway."

I know what it's like to go home after Sunday service in the afternoons and feel such a strong desire to see growth and fruit in our church, and yet be convinced we must be doing something wrong. I know that hurt, that internal struggle. I'm very familiar with it, but Jesus said, "Seek first the kingdom of God and his righteousness, and all these things will be added to you."[3] He didn't say seek man's approval first.

Beloved, God can do something miraculous with the person who is in the middle of nowhere—like David in the middle of Bethlehem. He can do something incredible with the one who has been left in obscurity—the one to whom He has delegated the care, nurture, and protection of a small flock of sheep. Remember nobody thought, out of all Jesse's sons, David would be the one Samuel anointed as king. David was out in the middle of nowhere, taking care of sheep, but something about his heart and the vow he made in his heart touched the heart of God so that God basically said, "I can use this young man."

You may not live in Bethlehem, but you may live in Kalamazoo or Timbuktu, and you feel frustrated, as if you're doing everything wrong. You may want to really go after the Presence of God but think, *If I really begin to push and develop prayer so that it becomes the center of all I do, I'm going to have to give up other things. I'm going to lose people. And I don't know if I can do this, let alone do it well.*

But if you will respond to the call of the voice of the Lord in this hour and say, "I will not give rest to my eyes. I will not crawl into my bed. I will not make anything else a priority in my church and my life—even if I lose it all—until I have brought back the Presence of the Lord and created a resting place for His Presence," God will meet you. He will show up, and He will transform people's lives.

This new order is what will change Millennials, Gen Z, and Gen Alpha—the very ones who have all the information at their fingertips yet don't have a sense of identity, purpose, belonging, or connection to the God of Abraham, Isaac, and Jacob. The order of David will beckon a dry and weary American church—the Body of Christ in a polarized nation—to come to an environment and say, "God is here, and I did not know it until now."

If we will set our hearts to be one of those tent poles from my dream—one of those tent poles the Lord is erecting all over America and even the world—I believe He will come and He "will draw all people" to Himself.[4] His resting place will become a resting place for the peoples of the earth. And that is what will bring revival and reformation.

---

1. Acts 6:4
2. E. M. Bounds, *Preacher and Prayer* (Mansfield Centre, CT: Martino Publishing, 2014), 13.
3. Matthew 6:33
4. John 12:32

NINE
THE NECESSITY OF PRAYER

PRAYER IS essential to every believer, and it is essential to the Church. Church models built around seekers, movements built around celebrities, and church services built around style have been the norm in America. Sadly, we've exchanged the manifest Presence of God and His miracle-working power for pragmatism and practicality. We've built around the void of God's absence rather than around the Presence of His Person.

But God is giving us this divine transition to revisit what Jesus said about His house—about the place where He dwells. He said His house is supposed to be "called a house of prayer."[1]

Jesus didn't relegate prayer to the back room or the prayer room, for that matter. Prayer should be so present and prevalent in the house of God that His house is known as a dwelling place of prayer. God should dwell in His house, and prayer should dwell there with Him!

The early church understood the necessity of prayer. After Jesus ascended to the Father, the disciples and many others went back to Jerusalem and gathered in the upper room,

> where they were staying, Peter and John and James and Andrew, Philip and Thomas, Bartholomew and Matthew, James the son of Alphaeus and Simon the Zealot and Judas the son of James. All these with one accord were devoting themselves to prayer, together with the women and Mary the mother of Jesus, and his brothers.
>
> ACTS 1:13–14

After they saw Jesus ascend to the Father, you would have thought that the disciples would have come up with the greatest evangelism strategy ever to fulfill the Great Commission. But they didn't do that. You may have even thought they would have run about the city recounting in hyperbolic detail how they saw Jesus flying up into the sky when "a cloud took him out of their sight."[2] But they didn't do that either. And they didn't even spin tales about seeing the two men who "stood by them in white robes" and what the guys had said.[3] No, the very first thing that Jesus' followers did was return to the upper room and devote themselves to prayer.

It's so striking to me how Jesus basically birthed the Church in an upper room with His followers praying. He had told them before His Ascension, "You will receive power when the Holy Spirit has come upon you, and you will be my witnesses in Jerusalem and in all Judea and Samaria, and to the end of the earth."[4] He knew they would need power for their mission. And to receive that power, these disciples gathered together to pray and wait for ten days.

Imagine a ten-day prayer meeting after having just seen Jesus in person after His resurrection. That's not a bad Bible college to go to if you're one of the apostles. I mean, you spend forty days with the resurrected Son of the living God, walking in and out of your upper room, where He is teaching you about the Kingdom of God. That's not a bad theological degree to have.

The Bible tells us there were about 500 people to whom Jesus appeared after His resurrection—after already having appeared to the women, Peter, the other disciples, and His brothers. Yet there were only 120 in the upper room that were praying on the Day of Pentecost when the power of heaven came and met the Church. It makes me want to know what happened to the other 380 people. It would be a terrible thing if you were the one who showed up to the prayer meeting for the first nine days and thought, *It looks like nothing is going to happen,* and then you went to Costco or someplace else on day ten. You find out later that fire fell from heaven on day ten. You wouldn't want to be that guy who then heard from the 120, "Oh, you should have been at that prayer meeting. It was incredible! The fire and wind of God came. He filled the entire place. Now, what were you doing?"

"I was renewing my membership at Costco and grabbing a rotisserie chicken for dinner."

No, nobody would want to be that guy with the other 379 who went AWOL.

"AND WHEN THEY HAD PRAYED"

The Church was birthed in the place of prayer. It's where God met them. It's where God ignited them with the power of the Holy Spirit. And when we move on in Acts 3 and 4, what we find is the Church as it began to thrive and explode, even in one of the most difficult cultural environments that you can imagine. The very same people who had crucified and conspired against Jesus hadn't changed their minds about Him. The only thing that had changed was the Church had been filled with power and sent on mission by Jesus.

The Church was still being persecuted. The followers of Christ were still being hunted down. They were still being ostracized. They were still hated. As a matter of fact, the persecution was becoming so bad that, later in Acts 9, we read about this guy named Saul, who was "still breathing threats and murder against the disciples of the Lord."[5] He even had picked up some letters from the high priest, "so that if he found any belonging to the Way, men or women, he might bring them bound to Jerusalem."[6]

Sometimes, we have in our minds this idea that the early church exploded on the scene in a very religious and very welcoming, pro-Jesus environment, but when we accurately read the Scriptures, we discover the Church was in a very antichrist, persecuting, pressurized environment. It was in this environment that the Church began to come alive, thrive, and explode.

In Acts 4, for example, Peter and John had just healed the lame man and "were speaking to the people" when "the priests and the captain of the temple and the Sadducees came upon them, greatly annoyed because they were teaching the people and proclaiming in Jesus the resurrection from the dead."[7] Peter and John were arrested as a result and held "in custody until the next day."[8] Something good did come out of their arrest, however. Peter "filled with the Holy Spirit" was able to declare with authority:

> Rulers of the people and elders, if we are being examined today concerning a good deed done to a crippled man, by what means this man has been healed, let it be known to all of you and to all the people of Israel that by the name of Jesus Christ of Nazareth, whom you crucified, whom God raised up from the dead—by him this man is standing before you well. This Jesus is the stone

that was rejected by you, the builders, which has become the cornerstone. And there is salvation in no one else, for there is no other name under heaven given among men by which we must be saved.

ACTS 4:8–12

Peter preached the unadulterated gospel to the leaders, and it blew their minds because the leaders recognized that Peter and John were "uneducated, common men."[9] The leaders basically had nothing to say in response except to warn Peter and John not to speak in the name of Jesus anymore. The leaders threatened Peter and John about what would happen if they continued to preach in the authority and power of Christ. Amazingly, Peter and John were released "because of the people, for all were praising God for what had happened. For the man on whom this sign of healing was performed was more than forty years old."[10] Nothing could hinder the spread of the gospel—not even persecution! To the contrary, persecution was advancing Christ's message of hope.

But what happened next? What did Peter and John do upon their release? They ran back to their place of prayer among their friends and cried out to God with them:

"Sovereign Lord, who made the heaven and the earth and the sea and everything in them, who through the mouth of our father David, your servant, said by the

Holy Spirit, 'Why did the Gentiles rage, and the peoples plot in vain? The kings of the earth set themselves, and the rulers were gathered together, against the Lord and against his Anointed'—for truly in this city there were gathered together against your holy servant Jesus, whom you anointed, both Herod and Pontius Pilate, along with the Gentiles and the peoples of Israel, to do whatever your hand and your plan had predestined to take place. And now, Lord, look upon their threats and grant to your servants to continue to speak your word with all boldness, while you stretch out your hand to heal, and signs and wonders are performed through the name of your holy servant Jesus." And when they had prayed, the place in which they were gathered together was shaken, and they were all filled with the Holy Spirit and continued to speak the word of God with boldness.

ACTS 4:24–31

I love that they quoted a psalm of David—Psalm 2—in their prayer. They were going back to their foundations, to the words of a man who inaugurated the new order of worship and priestly ministry. King David had experienced firsthand the violent pushback of people and kings and rulers against the Most High, and he understood prophetically that the Messiah would be railed against as well. These early Christians were basically telling the Lord, "The leaders conspired against You. They crucified You, and now, they're conspiring against us. God, we're asking You right now in this city to move. Would You stretch out Your hand and do miracles, Lord? We need You to show up in our city!"

Just as they completed their prayer, we read in verse 31, "And when they had prayed, the place in which they were gathered together was shaken, and they were all filled with the Holy Spirit and continued to speak the word of God with boldness." That's powerful! "And when they had prayed," God responded. He shook the place. He filled them all with the Holy Spirit again. And they left there boldly sharing the Word of God!

Church, what would happen today if we prayed? What would happen if God's house was known as a house of prayer? The book of Acts, that's what! In chapter one, we talked about how the book of Acts is happening again in other countries of the earth and how we need that to happen here in America. If we want the book of Acts to happen here, the Church must become a house of prayer.

That great and fiery preacher Leonard Ravenhill (1907–1994) said this: "Let the fire go out in the boiler room of the Church, and the place will still look smart and clean, but it will be cold. The Prayer Room is the boiler room for its spiritual life."[11] We don't want to "look smart and clean" yet "be cold." We need heat in the furnace. We need prayer in God's house—prayer that calls for God to be glorified, for His will to be accomplished, for souls to be saved, for signs, wonders, and miracles to erupt!

1. Matthew 21:13; Mark 11:17
2. Acts 1:9
3. Acts 1:10–11
4. Acts 1:8
5. Acts 9:1
6. Acts 9:2
7. Acts 4:1–2
8. Acts 4:3
9. Acts 4:13
10. Acts 4:21–22
11. Leonard Ravenill. Quotefancy.com, 2023. https://quotefancy.com/quote/852491/Leonard-Ravenhill-Let-the-fires-go-out-in-the-boiler-room-of-the-church-and-the-place/, accessed March 28, 2023.

TEN

A PRAYING AND WORSHIPPING CHURCH

JANE and I were living in Grand Rapids after having moved back from Kansas City, Missouri. In Kansas City, we had served as youth pastors, and when we came back to our home church in Grand Rapids, we felt called to plant a church. It was 1996, and church planting wasn't cool. It wasn't in vogue like it is today. Church planting in the 2020s may be the new missiology in that everyone wants to plant a church to reach people. But that's not how it was when Jane and I felt God leading us to start a work in Richland, Michigan.

In fact, in 1996, there were only a few books on church planting. One was Rick Warren's book titled *The Purpose-Driven Church.* I purchased and read that. Another book was by Ted Haggard, called *Primary Purpose: Making It Hard for People to Go to Hell from Your City.* That was an incredible book. And the third book I read was called *About Father's House,* which was by one of my mentors, Pastor Loren Covarrubias. He wrote about planting Mt. Zion Church in Clarkston, Michigan. I read those three books to help us navigate planting a church.

I knew that God had called us to plant a church, but Jane and I were just barely in our mid-twenties. Though God had placed a region and even a city upon our hearts—namely, Richland, Michigan—we didn't have any people. We didn't have any money. We didn't have a building. And we didn't have a clue about what we were doing. What we did have was this burning conviction that God had called us to plant a church in a certain place.

I remember the first time we drove out toward Richland. Jane and I saw the water tower and that was about it. We wondered if we were going in the right direction. "Is this it?" we questioned. Compared to the thriving metropolis it is today, there was nothing there except the tower, a flashing light, a post office, maybe one dog, and 1,400 people. But God had given us this city, and that meant we would start working toward accepting the call to the region.

That summer of 1996, Jane and I began to do all the things we were reading about doing to start a church. We built a core team, first pulling together some people to pray. We cast vision with that team. We found a place to rent for meetings. And we bought Tupperware tubs to store things in, borrowing a red trailer to pull behind a fifteen-passenger van that we used to cart around the stuff in the tubs we would need to conduct services.

The community high school rented their auditorium/cafeteria area to us. I called it a "cafetorium" myself because it wasn't quite either an auditorium or a cafeteria. Cafetorium seemed most appropriate. There was a bit of a problem, though, when you entered the cafetorium. The sports teams for the school were called the Blue Devils, and over the entrance into the cafetorium, there was this sign that said, "Welcome to the Devil's Den." Perfect signage, don't you think, for a church plant?

While we were making all our preparation, there was a battle taking place in my heart. I was struggling with all those things a young leader struggles with—some anxiety and fear, some real insecurity, and several questions about what happens if I fail or it doesn't work. Or worse yet, I had true concerns about what happens if it all blows up! *What if no one comes?* was the question that kept repeating itself in my mind. The reality was I didn't know how to do what we were doing, and that was pretty scary for me.

One day, I was driving in my Pontiac Grand Am down US 131 from Baldwin, Michigan, to Grand Rapids. I had left Jane and the kids at her parents' cottage in Baldwin and was returning to our hometown. I was pretty desperate that day and was praying those desperate kind of prayers. I was spiritually at a crossroads, scared I didn't have what it took to do what I knew God had called us to do. And that had started to wear me down to where I was beginning to wonder if I had taken on more than I was capable of doing. My prayers went something like this, "God, You got to help me! What am I supposed to do? How are we supposed to do this? I don't know if I can go through with this. If You don't do something, this isn't going to work."

What happened next can only be described as an incredible encounter with Jesus. He made Himself, His very Presence, manifest in my car. He was there, right there, and I heard Him say, "Lee, build a praying and worshipping church—a praying and worshipping church that will build the Body of Christ—and you will reach the nations." That became our mission when there wasn't even anybody in our church. We hadn't even had one service yet, but Jesus showed up in my car and gave me our mandate.

"BUILD A PRAYING AND WORSHIPPING CHURCH"

Well, we had our word from God, our mission was set, and I was strengthened in my faith and fortified in my resolve to do what He had told me. Like David, I made a hard right toward Zion, and I haven't regretted it.

Jane and I experienced all the ups and downs of doing a church plant. I remember we had seventy people on our first Sunday! It was awesome! But then the next week we had a Gideon's revival. Do you know what a Gideon's revival is? It's when you grow backwards. We went from seventy to fifty people. Oh, and on our first Sunday, I had someone come up to me and say, "We're really excited about this church plant!"

"That's great," I said, happy to hear such an encouraging response to our first service.

Then the guy asked, "When do we get to meet the pastor?"

A bit embarrassed, I replied, "Well, that's me."

"Oh," he said a little embarrassed himself, "I thought you were the youth pastor."

I was twenty-five and had tried so hard to look older. I mean, I had put on the suit and tie. Remember those days? But it didn't work.

Then on the second Sunday, I had another person come up to me and say, "Well, we just can't go to a church with somebody as young as you leading it."

I don't know why they had to say anything to me at all. But between their statement and dropping twenty people in attendance after one week, I was very discouraged though still committed to the mission. We were meeting in the Devil's Den, I—the young preacher—still had acne, and people were telling me they had a problem with my age. And there was nothing I could do about any of those things at the moment.

I'm so thankful for the word God gave us and the heart conviction that He strengthened for us, directing us to build a praying and worshipping church. We started to go after that mandate over twenty-five years ago, and it still burns inside Jane and me. And our conviction is that we're not supposed to be the exception to what a church should be in this hour. No, we believe this type of church is supposed to be the rule. In fact, that's what bringing the Presence of God back centerstage means. It means having churches that pray and worship like David did. It means having churches that pray, worship, and share the Word of God like the early church did.

What every city needs is a praying and worshipping Church. What an insecure world needs is a praying and worshipping Church. What a confused generation needs is a praying and worshipping Church.

Today, worship has become cool. It's become a major part of our meetings. But it's also become more technologically and platform driven, where those gathered in the congregation act more like spectators in an audience than priests ministering unto their Lord and Savior.

God wants priests ministering to Him in song and dance, priests offering up prayers as incense before Him, because He has called us "a royal priesthood, a holy nation, a people for his own possession . . . proclaim[ing] the excellencies of him who called [us] out of darkness into his marvelous light."[1] He wants worshippers on the platform, not rockstars. He wants singers and musicians actively singing and playing their instruments, making "His praise glorious."[2] Jesus said, the Father is looking for those who will worship Him "in spirit and truth."[3]

While worship has grown in popularity, prayer has not been platform driven but shut up in some back room in the church. God wants His Church to be a praying Church, not just so that we pray some nice little prayers, but so that He can shake us and shake the earth around us like He did the early church in Acts 4. He wants a praying Church to be like a spiritual nuclear reactor inside a city or spiritual territory. If He can get His Church to pray and to believe their prayer—their intercession—literally changes atmospheres and environments, it will lead to a spiritual critical mass that releases a mushroom cloud of heavenly supernatural activity in a region. And that will transform a people, a city, a generation, and even a nation.

---

1. 1 Peter 2:9
2. Psalm 66:2 NKJV
3. John 4:23

ELEVEN
PRAYER THAT GOES NUCLEAR

SOMETHING HAPPENED when the early church began to experience great pressure from the culture surrounding it. When cultural dissonance and spiritual pressure increased, the early church grew hungry and desperate. And prayer was its response. But let's talk about cultural dissonance and spiritual pressure for a moment.

Spiritual pressure is what we all experience when the culture around us is increasing in sin and darkness, when it is growing more antichrist in its actions and beliefs. This difference in culture doesn't only produce pressure, however; it produces dissonance. Cultural dissonance is the clashing or tension that arises as the outside culture of the world becomes more different than the inside culture of the Kingdom of God. So, both spiritual pressure and cultural dissonance are produced by the world getting darker and sin increasing while the Church continues to grow numerically and spiritually (e.g., in purity, holiness, righteousness, etc.). Let's use a chart to better explain this.

ACTS 4: A NUCLEAR REACTION OF SPIRITUAL PROPORTIONS

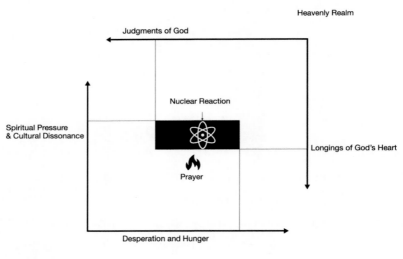

We can see in the chart above that there are more things going on than spiritual pressure, cultural dissonance, desperation, and hunger. There are things going on coming from the heavenly realm—namely, the judgments of God and the longings of God's heart. On the left and bottom sides of the chart, we have scales that represent the Church in the earthly realm dealing with spiritual pressure and cultural dissonance that lead to the Church experiencing desperation and hunger. And on the top and left sides, we have scales that represent God in the heavenly realm with His judgments and longings.

The judgments of God are one of the most under-taught aspects of the Bible. God is still Judge, and He must judge unrighteousness. Isaiah 2:4 says God will "judge between the nations," and we know according to Psalm 96:10 that He "will judge the peoples with equity." We also know that the apostle Peter wrote, "For it is time for judgment to begin at the household of God; and if it begins with us, what will be the outcome for those who do not obey the gospel?"[1] Revelation 15:7 tells us about the seven angels that are given seven bowls by one of the four living creatures. The bowls are "full of the wrath of God," and they will be poured out on the earth.

But thank God for His mercy because we have on the righthand side of the chart the scales that represent God's longing heart for His Church. The dream in God's heart, the longing within Him, is for communion and union with us, His people. After all, He will have a bride who is without blemish and in no need of ironing.[2]

So, the heavenly realm scales converge on our chart and form a large rectangle, and the earthly realm scales do as well. Now, taken as a whole, all the scales on the chart can illustrate how the Church is brought to the point of critical mass, where there is enough fissile material present to generate a spiritual nuclear chain reaction. When these two scales converge, it's representative of what Jesus said regarding our praying that His Kingdom come and His "will be done on earth as it is in heaven."[3] When all four scales intersect, a heavenly supernatural reaction—like that which happened in Acts 4—can take place, that is, if the Church prays and worships in response. I'm actually calling that a nuclear reaction of spiritual proportions. You can see that intersection represented in the black rectangle in the center of the chart. And you can see the fire of prayer is present to trigger the reaction.

Now, when we look at the bottom scale picturing the response of the Church to that dissonance and spiritual pressure, we find that desperation and hunger increase as well. Let's say that, if the dissonance and spiritual pressure move up a ways on the scale, then the Church's response in hunger and desperation will also move up. In other words, there's a positive correlation between the two scales. If over the last twenty years, we've gone up in spiritual pressure and cultural dissonance, then the Church's hunger and desperation have moved up correspondingly until they have met and formed that rectangle that we see in our chart.

For everything that happens on earth to which the Church has a reaction, there is God who in His omniscience, foreknowledge, and timing is ready to meet His Church and the earth with His Presence and judgments respectively. His wrath "is revealed from heaven against all ungodliness and unrighteousness of men, who by their unrighteousness suppress the truth."[4] As spiritual pressure and cultural dissonance are increasing—the nations raging and the rulers taking counsel against God and conspiring to overthrow God's righteous ways—God's judgments, the bowls of His wrath, begin to fill.[5] Again, when the cultural dissonance and spiritual pressure, and the Church's response in hunger and desperation go up, the bowls of God's judgments begin to fill.

But what else happens is God's longing for His people grows closer to being manifested. In His longing, God's heart cries out to the depths of our hearts, and we can begin to experience what David described in Psalm 42:7— "Deep calls to deep at the roar of your waterfalls; all your breakers and your waves have gone over me." The Church, then, instead of becoming bitter, instead of looking to other things as the solution to our hunger and desperation, allows hunger to increase because it will enlarge our hearts for God's heart to meet ours. And what happens then is, suddenly, we come to a holy intersection between heaven's agenda and earth's response. It's here in this intersection, in that solid center rectangle on the chart, where we begin to see a spiritual nuclear reaction as we pray and worship God together.

Really, this all is a picture of what happened in Acts 4. It's a reaction called critical mass. When fissile material— nuclear material—reaches a point of instability, it sets off a chain reaction of nuclear explosion. That's how nuclear science works. And what we read about in Acts 2 and, more specifically, in Acts 4 is a perfect picture of this spiritual critical mass.

1. 1 Peter 4:17
2. See Ephesians 5:27.
3. Matthew 6:10
4. Romans 1:18
5. See Psalm 2:1–6.

TWELVE
ACTS 4 REALITY

I BELIEVE with all my heart that we are at a critical mass point in America and in the other nations of the earth. We are at that intersection we discussed in the last chapter, and something is about to explode like it did in Acts 4. Friend, I believe we're about to experience an Acts 4 reality if the Church will pray and bring the Presence of God back front-and-center.

Just think about what happened in the book of Acts during a time when they didn't have trains, planes, or automobiles. They didn't have Bible colleges. They didn't have Instagram or Twitter accounts. They didn't have the printing press let alone the internet. No smartphones or laptops. What the early church did have was the Presence of God, and the first Christians had within their hearts a holy desperation that led them to pray. Prayer was the early church's default setting.

When everything was going haywire, these believers prayed. When they needed a miracle, they prayed. When they met together, they prayed. When they were trying to figure out answers to theological issues that were raised because of cultural dissonance, they prayed. When their leaders or fellow disciples were imprisoned, they prayed—they interceded.

Though it might not be as evident in a cursory reading of Acts 4, once you begin to put the facts together that are present within the chapter, you see a mushroom cloud forming, telling you there was a holy detonation that took place in the city of Jerusalem. That explosion billowed out from Jerusalem to Judea, to Samaria, and to the uttermost parts of the world, which is what Jesus had said would happen after the Holy Spirit had come upon them.[1] I propose to you the only reason the Church is here today in multiple nations of the world is because 2,000 years ago there was a spiritual atomic reaction that took place in the city limits of Jerusalem. The Church then was under the most intense pressure, but that released the force of God's favor and blessing on the Great Commission through the Church.

I also believe each of us are in the Church today because someone prayed. As John Wesley said,

God does nothing but in answer to prayer: and even they who have been converted to God without praying for it themselves, (which is exceeding rare,) were not without the prayers of others. Every new victory which a soul gains is the effect of a new prayer.[2]

We don't even know the prayers that have been prayed over our lives—prayers that have impacted our lives in many ways. I think, when we get to heaven, one of the things that may shock us the most is how much fruit there actually is as a result of our prayers that we chalked up as unanswered because we didn't get a Western Union wire from an angel that said, "Okay, you prayed. Here's the result." I wonder, what would happen if the Church became convinced that our prayers really matter?

PRAYER IN OUR CONTEXT

I've been thinking a lot about prayer in the context of where the Church is at today. We are living in unprecedented and unpredictable times with a new level of spiritual pressure that has been unleashed. It's interesting to watch how the Church responds to this pressure. It makes me think of other times in our history when the pressure was not as great or even existent for that matter.

For quite a while in the West, the Church lived in what can be described as a zero gravity environment. Gravity is the force that pushes us down toward the center of the earth. If you or I were to get into one of the SpaceX rockets, and we were to shoot up to the International Space Station, we would be in a zero gravity environment. Some of the astronauts have lived in that kind of environment for months on end. You've probably seen video of them floating around the station, you know, squirting out their toothpaste and trying to catch it on their toothbrush. Everything just floats around in "the air" because there is zero gravity. Yet in this environment, the astronauts' minds are still sharp. They're still moving around, but everything they do is without the resistance or pressure from gravity. Their muscles actually weaken. It's incredible to think how God designed our physical bodies to respond to gravity, where we automatically regenerate and rejuvenate our muscular systems on a daily basis without even knowing it —because just standing up and getting out of bed is pushing against the pressure of gravity. But if we ever were to get out of a gravitational environment, we would see the effects on our muscles from them not having to resist the pressure. Our muscles would begin to die in such an environment.

The Church has been living in a spiritual space station for about three decades, in my opinion, where we've had zero pressure on us as followers of Jesus because the moral lines of the Church were running parallel with the morally accepted belief systems of the modern culture. America wasn't a Christian nation in that everyone was a believer and follower of Christ, but at least we had Judeo-Christian principles that "kind of" ran in the same direction. If you were a pastor in the modern period of American life, you were highly regarded and respected. In fact, if you didn't attend church in some local cultures or communities, you were not offered certain jobs because the people hiring wouldn't trust you. They didn't see you as a moral and upright citizen. That simply was the way things were in modern America. That used to be our reality.

Compare that to the post-modern times we live in today. We read about people from major urban populations who are asked questions about religious extremism, for example. They're asked in surveys how they would classify people who attend church every single week. What these surveys have shown is many of these urban dwellers see consistent church attendance as religious extremism. You and I, in their estimation, are religious extremists! So, now, the Church has come back into a gravitational environment, and we're feeling pressure. For some of us, it's the very first time we've experienced this. And for others, like our children or grandchildren, it's been the experience of their entire existence.

Some of us think we're experiencing persecution, but it actually is spiritual warfare at this juncture in time. It is moving toward persecution, however. All the pressure we're now living in that's arising in our country's culture is growing more and more antagonistic to Christ. We're at the end of the age when the beginning of sorrows and the birth pangs are increasing, and man, how we are feeling it! We're feeling the spiritual pressure and the cultural dissonance—all the stuff we've been talking about in the last few chapters. We even feel it within the Church as people are walking away from the Faith. They're making Jesus in their own image instead of recognizing they were created in His.

Furthermore, we are deconstructing the Bible. We're customizing the Bible to fit our cultural preferences and our pet sins. If we're going to live godly lives in Christ Jesus, Paul said this:

> My persecutions and sufferings that happened to me at Antioch, at Iconium, and at Lystra—which persecutions I endured; yet from them all the Lord rescued me. Indeed, all who desire to live a godly life in Christ Jesus will be persecuted, while evil people and impostors will go on from bad to worse, deceiving and being deceived.
>
> 2 TIMOTHY 3:11–13

The bottom line is we will suffer persecution. What is that? It's pressure, but can I tell you that it's nothing new for the majority of the Church in other lands? The majority of the Church in other countries has been in a gravitational environment, where the pressure of persecution is all that they've ever known. And in their hunger and desperation, the persecuted believers in these nations are seeing crazy, wonderful things take place as they cry out to God, as they revere and honor His Presence.

I've had people ask me, "Why don't we see more power? Why don't we see the miraculous healings and the signs and the wonders we hear about in Iran or China?" Well, we've not experienced the level of spiritual pressure and cultural dissonance that produces great hunger and desperation. And if God were to release the power and miraculous upon us without our being in a similar state to our persecuted brothers and sisters, I believe it would destroy us. Why? Because what we would try and do in our consumer culture is merchandise it. We would try to package it. We would trademark and brand it. We would try to control it. It would generate in our consumerism and celebrity culture even more celebrities and Christian superstars.

Some of the most prayer-filled, most godly, most faith-filled people I have ever met or known are living in Third World nations, and nobody will ever see them. Nobody will ever recognize them. Nobody will ever know them on earth as the mighty men and women—mighty servants of God— who have laid down their lives in prayer and worship. But heaven knows them.

We live in the context of twenty-first-century America, in what Timothy Keller calls a "post-everything United States."[3] America today is post-culture, post-ideological, post-modern, and post-Christian. But I'm convinced this is a context for prayer. It's a context for bringing the Presence of God as the precedent for all we do. It's a context for an Acts 4 reality—I believe it with all my heart!

We have identity and gender confusion becoming pervasive. We have just under half of Gen Z now identifying on the LGBTQIA spectrum. We have anger and rioting in our streets. People are fighting against each other on subway platforms and in subway cars, in air terminals and on airplanes, and in homes among families. Violence and bitter hatred are breaking out all across America. We have social media that is a toxic virus. All it is doing is revealing how sick and corrupt we have become. Religious liberties are under attack. People are calling right wrong and wrong right. All these things are working a great instability—perfect conditions for an Acts 4-type nuclear explosion—if the Church prays, that is.

Please hear me. All of this is *good news* because the conditions in our country today are very similar to those the early church was experiencing, those documented in the book of Acts. This is our opportunity to cry out to God as His people. If we will give no rest to our eyes and no stopping to our prayers, we will see what happened in Acts 4 happen in our country.

---

1. See Acts 1:8.
2. John Wesley, *A Plain Account of Christian Perfection* (New York: Lane & Scott, 1850), 157.
3. Timothy Keller, "Post-everythings," Westminster Theological Seminary/Articles and Publications, https://students.wts.edu/resources/articles/keller_posteverythings.html/, accessed April 3, 2023.

THIRTEEN
WHEN THE CHURCH PRAYS

THE BOOK of Acts is the story of God's Spirit being poured out between prayer meetings. Looking once again at Acts 4:31, we see that certain things happened to the early church "when they had prayed." If we will pray, I believe we will see the following five things happen.

THE PRESENCE OF THE LORD SHAKES THE CHURCH

First of all, when the Church prays, the Presence of the Lord shakes the Church. You see, God doesn't want His Church to be shaken by the things that are happening in the earth. Hebrews 12:26–29 affirms this:

> At that time his voice shook the earth, but now he has promised, "Yet once more I will shake not only the earth but also the heavens." This phrase, "Yet once more,"

indicates the removal of things that are shaken—that is, things that have been made—in order that the things that cannot be shaken may remain. Therefore let us be grateful for receiving a kingdom that cannot be shaken, and thus let us offer to God acceptable worship, with reverence and awe, for our God is a consuming fire.

Friend, we are receiving a Kingdom that cannot be shaken. God has promised us that, so God doesn't want us shaken by the things that are happening in the earth or by the things that will happen in the future.

As we approach the return of the Lord, we know pressure is going to increase. Spiritual warfare is going to ramp up. If you think it's tough today, just wait. Today will seem so much easier than what we will experience then. But God doesn't want us to be shaken by those days or the things that take place then. He does, however, want us to be shaken by His Presence like the prophet Isaiah was shaken in his vision of the Lord.

In the year that King Uzziah died I saw the Lord sitting upon a throne, high and lifted up; and the train of his robe filled the temple. Above him stood the seraphim. Each had six wings: with two he covered his face, and with two he covered his feet, and with two he flew. And one called to another and said: "Holy, holy, holy is the Lord of hosts; the whole earth is full of his glory!" And the foundations of the thresholds shook at the voice of him who called, and the house was filled with smoke. And I said: "Woe is me! For I am lost; for I am a man of unclean lips, and I dwell in the midst of a people of unclean lips; for my eyes have seen the King, the Lord of hosts!"

ISAIAH 6:1–5

In his vision, Isaiah was shaken, and the foundations of the temple were shaken as well by the Presence of the Lord. It seems similar to what happened to those gathered together in Acts 4, where they were shaken, as was the place in which they were praying. And when we pray, we will be shaken, too, and His house will be shaken as His Presence permeates the atmosphere.

In 1988–89, I was a senior in high school, and in our youth group in Grand Rapids, we had Wednesday night services. We were experiencing revival in those days, though we didn't necessarily call it that at the time. We had started around twenty-five different campus ministries, and many of our friends were getting saved. There were 200–300 high school kids attending Wednesday nights to worship and pray.

In September of 1988, at around 7:30 p.m., we were having our youth group gathering and were worshipping together. I can remember my buddy Tom Lares leading worship on the keys, and as we were singing, suddenly, the entire building began to shake! It was so intense the windows actually rattled as a result. Then all kinds of stuff started shaking—including us! We all looked at each other in shock as we trembled together.

Later on, we discovered that we had experienced an actual earthquake. In fact, it was one of the only earthquakes ever recorded to have taken place in the Midwest. It just so happened to take place at the perfect time on Wednesday night when we were gathered together, worshipping the Lord. I'm convinced that our worship stirred God to shake us, the building, and our corner of the earth.

God wants to shake the Church much like Isaiah was shaken because the physical shaking of the building is nothing compared to what it does to the soul. When the Church prays, it shakes and awakens something deep within us. It rouses us out of our spiritual slumber, causing our eyes to open and see Jesus. And when we see Him in His holiness, we are convicted of sin, and our hearts cry out for forgiveness and help—for more of Him.

Church, if we begin to pray and call on His name during these times of great pressure and difficulty, the Lord will shake us and awaken us to the beauty of His holiness. And as 2 Corinthians 3:18 tells us, when we behold Him, we will be "transformed into the same image from one degree of glory to another." Seeing Him high and lifted up and seated upon the throne will shake us to the core, shake us to see His beauty, shake us to experience His holiness. I'm reminded of something A. W. Tozer wrote:

What God in His sovereignty may yet do on a world-scale I do not claim to know. But what He will do for the plain man or woman who seeks His face I believe I do know and can tell others. Let any man turn to God in earnest, let him begin to exercise himself unto godliness, let him seek to develop his powers of spiritual receptivity by trust and obedience and humility, and the results will exceed anything he may have hoped in his leaner and weaker days.[1]

THE CHURCH IS EMBOLDENED

The second thing that happens when the Church prays is the Church is emboldened. A praying Church becomes a bold Church. You see, boldness isn't going to come to you and me through our having a better grasp on apologetics, though we should know how to give a defense for the gospel we preach. And boldness isn't going to come to us by our having a certain number of followers on social media that we believe give us some influence or the ability to say certain things. That's not how boldness is ever going to come to us, the Church. Neither is boldness going to come to us because of whom we know, because of the size of our church, nor because of the stability of our finances. *Boldness is going to come when our lives intersect with the Presence of God.*

The early church "continued to speak the word of God with boldness" because the place where they were gathered was shaken, they were shaken, and the Holy Spirit filled them.[2] Do you know what the Church needs more of than anything today? *The Church needs bold Christians empowered by the Holy Spirit of God.* We need boldness because the enemy wants to silence us. The spirit of Jezebel in this generation wants to silence the prophetic voice of Elijah and intimidate you—to cause you to run and hide—when you were called to be a prophetic voice of hope and salvation and truth.

One of the indicators of the Great Awakenings, the Azusa Street revival, and the Jesus Revolution was this boldness to witness, to share the Faith with people. Bold believers were intentional and direct in asking others, "Do you know about Jesus? Let me tell you my story." The most contagious way that people get saved is through other people whom they know, and even those they don't know, witnessing to them about who Jesus is and what He's done in their lives. And one of the greatest frustrations I've had with the American church over the last twenty to thirty years is we've become really good at evangelism, inviting people to church meetings, as opposed to boldly telling them what Jesus has done in our lives.

Now, I know we need to invite people to church services, and we need to give altar calls to provide a place for those who don't know Jesus to respond to the gospel message in our services. I love that. We want to continue to provide such opportunities. However, we must get back to a place where the Church is filled with the Holy Spirit to such an extent that we can't help but tell people that Jesus is real, that He is alive, and that He saves to the uttermost! In fact, Jesus can save anyone—anyone whosoever.

We have a generation that needs the good news of the gospel of Jesus Christ. And can I just tell you that the gospel is not one option among many to receive eternal life? No, it's the only way to salvation and life eternal with God, for as Jesus said to Thomas, "I am the way, and the truth, and the life. No one comes to the Father except through me."[3]

What would happen in our cities if our churches were filled with believers who were bold in proclaiming the Word of God and were empowered by the Holy Spirit? What would happen in high schools if we had students who were so captivated by who Jesus is and what He has done in their lives that they were willing to be mocked and ridiculed just for saying Jesus is real and He saved them and changed their lives?

There are testimonies that will set people free. There are testimonies of people who will say, "I came out of this lifestyle. I came out of that addiction. I came out of this belief system, but Jesus has radically changed my life." We need those testimonies. We need those voices because otherwise even the Church gets lulled to sleep in believing, "Well, I really don't have a testimony to share about some wild kind of deliverance or life change. I love the Lord and have known Him since I was a child, but I'll just keep it to myself because, well, I don't have anything relatable to people today."

You need Jesus to be your personal Lord and Savior, but He is not supposed to be your private Lord and Savior to where you keep your testimony to yourself— your testimony of how He saved you and how He has walked with you and met you in your time of need. We are called to be bold in our witness. Why were the early believers bold in Acts 4? Because they had encountered Jesus. They had been with Jesus and had been filled with the Holy Spirit.

How are you going to preach Jesus to an antagonistic culture? How are you going to preach Jesus to people in a corporate world where money is their god and they're trying to climb the "corporate ladder" of success up to the top? How are you going to preach Jesus to people who have no religious background whatsoever?

Two or three years ago, pre-COVID-19, a young woman came up to me at the end of one of my messages. She was a college student. I had made reference to Noah's ark in my message, and she basically said to me, "That was a fascinating speech. Can you tell me who's the Noah guy you've been talking about?"

It really took me back for a moment. I remember saying, "Noah, you know, the guy who had the ark, like the boat where he put animals in, like two by two?"

"When did that happen? And, uh, how big was his boat?" she asked. She had never heard of Noah's ark. This young woman had absolutely no frame of reference for a simple Bible story like Noah's ark.

I talked to another woman on a different occasion who was about my age. She was saved in our church a few years ago, but she had no previous religious background, having been saved at the age of 48. She, too, had no biblical frame of reference. When she got saved, she started at ground zero and had no biblical literacy whatsoever.

Church, we must be emboldened to share the gospel. We cannot afford to be "ashamed of the gospel, for it is the power of God for salvation to everyone who believes, to the Jew first and also to the Greek."[4] We must share the gospel unabashedly, and we need Holy Ghost boldness to do so.

THE CHURCH IS UNIFIED

Third, when the Church prays, the Church is unified. In Acts 4:32, "the full number of those who believed were of one heart and soul." There is no more unifying force in the Church than when we pray together.

The devil understands this, so he will do anything and everything he can to keep us from praying in our churches. He will work hard to distract us from prayer, using even the good things that we are engaged in that are meant to advance the gospel. He will use church fundraisers, church programs, ministry outreaches, and ministry missions. Can I just tell you that the devil would have been fine with the early church trying to accomplish the Great Commission if that meant they did not pray in Jerusalem and wait for the power of the Holy Spirit? I mean, the devil would have been just fine with them doing that. Why? Because then they would have been ineffective. But thank God that didn't happen.

Instead, the early church was unified around the place of prayer. Brothers and sisters were praying and tarrying together when God poured out His Spirit on them. Their prayer unified them with heaven. And when we pray together as the Body of Christ, prayer will unify us with one another and with heaven.

Over the past twenty-plus years, as I have led every kind of prayer meeting you can lead, I've found that prayer is work. Don't misunderstand me. I've led prayer meetings that have been full of the Presence of God, where men, women, and young people were crying out to God as one voice and heart. But I've led a lot of hard prayer meetings, where it seemed as though the heavens were as brass and the people dead to rights.

I used to lead a men's prayer meeting at five in the morning, and I asked every man to show up. In the first couple of weeks, fifty men showed up. We had no music, no special lighting, nothing—just prayer. It was very dry as you can imagine. As a few weeks went by, thirty men then showed up. A week later, we had twenty men. Another week, fifteen guys came. By week six or so, I showed up at five, and one other guy did as well. He said to me, "Want to go get breakfast at Denny's?"

"Uh, well, I really think we should probably pray, but that sounds good. Let's go get breakfast," I replied.

I don't know if you've ever had an experience like that, but it's a very real scenario in churches when people are asked to show up for prayer without any accoutrements.

I also remember starting a young adult prayer meeting in what we called the upper room on Friday nights. This was years ago. When we first started meeting together, we were all in! I mean, we were going to pray until Jesus comes. Once again, however, young adults started dropping out each week until nobody else came, and then I thought to myself, *All right, well, that didn't work out so good.*

Then we got this idea to pray through the Tabernacle. So, we set up the room like the Tabernacle and got people to sign up and go through it. But we had something bizarre begin to happen. People came and prayed through it, but a few people started to stay in the building. They would hide under tables, and we didn't know they were there or what they were up to. It was odd. We had to stop doing that.

Crazy things happen at prayer meetings. That's all I'm saying. I also remember hosting Monday morning prayer meetings in downtown Kalamazoo at the Radiant City Center. Four homeless guys came in and sat in the back row. They actually started rolling joints in the middle of one of our prayer sets!

I can't tell you how many prayer meetings we've started as a church and how many prayer meetings we've stopped, but we've been committed to keep going after prayer. We keep pursuing a way forward to pray together as a local body because we understand the Church is called to be a house of prayer; we're supposed to be a people of prayer. That's part of our DNA. We haven't given up. And in our pursuit, we have come upon prayer times and offerings that work for us as a people. We want to see prayer become the spiritual nuclear reactor that sends power into our weakened meetings and unites our people around the Presence of God.

I promise you that the one constant I've seen and experienced as we've gone after prayer together is that it has unified us in our pursuit of the Presence of God. The unity that we've had in Radiant Church has been because we've just kept going after prayer.

And we continue to pursue prayer together. One size doesn't fit all. One type of prayer meeting isn't going to cut it. So, we keep trying different types of prayer meetings, different ways of coming together to pursue His Presence. We'll go through the awkward together because that's the rallying point—to go through it all together to become one people of one heart and one mind.

There's something else I want to share about prayer meetings. What will work for your church and your local body of believers may not be what works for us in Richland or Portage or Kalamazoo. The point is find what God has called you to as a local expression of His Church and do that. And keep trying different ways to gather for prayer, different times and locations to pray, and different prayer focuses. Do all you can to discover what God has called your local body to do. Go through the awkward and the odd until you find His path of prayer for your church because, as you do this, you will become unified. When you're unified in prayer around the Presence of God in the heart of your town or city, your church will begin to push back the darkness.

GOD RELEASES POWER THROUGH THE CHURCH

The fourth thing that happens when the Church prays is God releases power through us—great power! He also releases healings, signs, and wonders when we pray.

In Acts 4:29–30, when the people prayed, they asked:

Lord, look upon their threats and grant to your servants to continue to speak your word with all boldness, while you stretch out your hand to heal, and signs and wonders are performed through the name of your holy servant Jesus.

Immediately, in verse 31, we read they received the boldness they requested to "speak the word of God." But what about the power and the healing and the signs and the wonders?

If we look at the opening of the next chapter, chapter 5, we read about a fearful sign. It's that of the deaths of Ananias and Sapphira. They lied to the Holy Spirit about the "proceeds of the land" they had sold.[5] Ananias dropped dead at Peter's feet after he lied, and within three hours, so did his wife, Sapphira, for doing the same.[6] "And great fear came upon the whole church and upon all who heard of these things."[7]

Then, in Acts 5:12, we see that "many signs and wonders were regularly done among the people by the hands of the apostles." Signs and wonders were happening "regularly" as God released them through the apostles. What's more is we're also told in Acts 5:14–16,

> And more than ever believers were added to the Lord, multitudes of both men and women, so that they even carried out the sick into the streets and laid them on cots and mats, that as Peter came by at least his shadow might fall on some of them. The people also gathered from the towns around Jerusalem, bringing the sick and those afflicted with unclean spirits, and they were all healed.

Wow! "They were all healed"! This was all in answer to the prayer of the people in Acts 4.

When the Church prays, God releases power through the Church. We see this in nations like South Korea, Argentina, and India, for example. There is a strong correlation between praying churches and the manifestation of miracles, signs, and wonders. Even in America, wherever we see strong, praying churches, there will be an uptick in supernatural activity, miraculous power, and breakthrough among the people of both the church and the city or town in which it is located.

Why? Because God responds when the Church prays. He releases His mighty power through His praying people.

CITIES ARE CHANGED

Lastly, when the Church prays, cities are changed. Do you believe that prayer will change your city? If you believe this and others in your local church start to believe this—and you all pray together—you will see it happen!

I want to get this in our hearts. Intercessory prayer— standing in the gap for the loss, doing spiritual warfare, declaring truth, prophesying the word of the Lord, fighting "the good fight of the faith," exalting Jesus, and worshipping Him as a unified people—will change the spiritual atmosphere in your city.[8] It will open up the heavens over your city. We must get a vision of this so that our faith can tenaciously fight until we see the vision actualized before us.

There is no program we can insert into the life of the Church that will impact our cities in a powerful way. Prayer isn't a program. Prayer isn't a lifestyle either. Prayer, as I've said before, is part of our genetic code as His Church. It's in our DNA. When we bleed, we should bleed prayer. That's what the early church did in the book of Acts. Anytime any attack or any persecution came, the early church bled prayer. And that's what impacted the people and cities around them.

There was a man named Jeremiah Lanphier (1809–1898) who started out as a New York businessman, a cloth merchant to be exact, until he closed his business in 1857 to begin to work as a lay minister.[9] At the age of 48, he was hired to come on staff and start an evangelism program in Manhattan. As a way to begin, he held a prayer meeting at noon on September 23, 1857. The first prayer meeting he held was at the North Dutch Reform Church, "with an entrance on Fulton Street," just down the street from what is now the World Trade Center.[10] He printed out a hand-bill, which read, "[Wednesday] prayer meeting from 12 to 1 o'clock. Stop 5, 10 or 20 minutes, or the whole time, as your time admits."[11] The first person to join him in prayer was a half-hour late, but eventually, four other people joined him. These people were from five different denominations. The lunch hour prayer meetings continued and increased exponentially until "by the end of March every downtown New York church and public hall was filled to capacity, and ten thousand men were gathering daily for prayer."[12]

Other noontime prayer meetings erupted across America in cities like Chicago, Kansas City, St. Louis, and even Kalamazoo. J. Edwin Orr, "a student of the revival, estimated that perhaps as many as a million people were converted in 1858 and 1859, more than 3% of a contemporary United States population of less than thirty million."[13] Interestingly enough, Kalamazoo's first united prayer meeting during the revival of 1858 saw people present from four different denominations. "Four or five were saved that very first hour. Before the revival was over, there were nearly five hundred conversions in Kalamazoo."[14] The description of this revival in Kalamazoo is striking in that what it highlighted is the unity among the Church:

> The fourth great awakening was above all a revival of unity. Denominational backgrounds were forgotten. . . . Everyone prayed for everyone else. . . . People who had been prayed for by loved ones for years now surrendered their lives to Jesus.[15]

Only recently was I made aware of the Kalamazoo connection. We bought our downtown building, where we opened a prayer room in response to the vision that God had given us years ago to be a praying church. We didn't know at the time what had taken place in 1858. I have since surmised that, as far as I can tell, the prayer meeting held in 1858 probably took place in Bronson Park or in one of the churches in Bronson Park, which is less than a hundred feet from our prayer room.

I believe there are revival embers in my city from that revival. They're lying dormant under the surface of our city, as it were. The population of Kalamazoo in 1858 was about 10,000 people. So, 500 people saved in that revival would represent 5 percent of the population. Isn't it amazing that all these individuals from cities across America in 1858 came to Christ because one man determined he was going to intercede and call others to do the same? His prayer ignited in churches across America and changed the spiritual climate of our cities. God ignited a nuclear reaction of spiritual proportions in 1858 and brought the Church to a state of critical mass and released a revival that caused people to be swept into the Kingdom of God! May it happen again in America in our day.

---

1. A. W. Tozer, *The Pursuit of God* (Camp Hill, PA: Christian Publications, Inc., 1992), 66.
2. Acts 4:31
3. John 14:6
4. Romans 1:16
5. Acts 5:3
6. See Acts 5:7–10.
7. Act 5:11
8. 1 Timothy 6:12
9. "Jeremiah Lanphier," Wikipedia, last modified November 6, 2021, https://en.wikipedia.org/wiki/Jeremiah_Lanphier/accessed March 30, 2023. According to the first footnote of the Wikipedia entry of Jeremiah Lanphier, his "name is often spelled 'Lamphier', presumably because Samuel I. Prime, the first historian of the 1857–1858 revival, spelled [sic] that way."
10. "Jeremiah Lanphier," Wikipedia, last modified November 6, 2021, https://en.wikipedia.org/wiki/Jeremiah_Lanphier/accessed March 30, 2023.
11. Ibid.
12. Ibid.
13. Ibid.
14. Wesley L. Duel, *Revival Fire* (Grand Rapids, MI: Zondervan, 2018), 132.
15. Ibid.

FOURTEEN
PITCH A TENT

I BELIEVE God's heart is to infect us with a holy unction to pray. He would love to hear our hearts cry out, "God, I'm going to pray. I'm going to invite my family to pray. I'm going to be a part of building a family altar in my home and a corporate altar in my church. I'm going to invite my neighbors and people from other churches to pray. I'm going to invite my church to pray. And I'm going to worship You like You're on the throne, because You are! I'm going to prophesy over my home, neighborhood, church, and city that Your Kingdom is coming. And I'm not going to give rest to my eyes—I'm not going to crawl into my bed—until I find a resting place for You, Lord. Until my home and my church become a resting place for You."

Call some people together for a prayer meeting. Call your family. Call your friends. Call your church. Call the mighty men. Call the women of God. Call the passionate young people. Call the exuberant children. Call the incessant intercessors and say, "It's time for us to break up the fallow ground and seek the Lord. It's time to ask the Lord for rain in the season of rain.[1] It's time for us to get on the wall like watchmen over our cities and over this generation that God has assigned to us. It *is* time for us to pray."

Begin to declare, "I'm not going to stand back and watch hell build its tower! Not on my watch!"

If you and I will begin to pray, then I believe what happened in Acts 4:31–33 will happen to us:

And when they had prayed, the place in which they were gathered together was shaken, and they were all filled with the Holy Spirit and continued to speak the word of God with boldness. Now the full number of those who believed were of one heart and soul, and no one said that any of the things that belonged to him was his own, but they had everything in common. And with great power the apostles were giving their testimony to the resurrection of the Lord Jesus, and great grace was upon them all.

Do you believe with me that what happened when they prayed can happen when we pray? Think about it.

What would happen if instead of reading, "And when they prayed," you read, "And when I prayed," or "And when my church prayed"? What would happen in your city if you were shaken and filled with boldness—if you and other believers in your city were unified as one heart and soul? How would your city be affected?

IT'S TIME TO PRAY

It's time for us to pray. It's time to pitch a tent. It's time for us to call on heaven and say, "Here we are. We're hammering some tent pegs into the ground right here in our city. We're saying, 'Lord, erect Your tent. Let Your glory cover our nation and start right here in our city!'"

That's the answer—the antidote—my friend, to the virus of consumer Christianity. Bringing the Presence back centerstage in our culture and houses of vibrant prayer and "spirit and truth" worship is what will bring back the power of God to the American church. We must never forget that the Presence of God is "the most holy and necessary practice in our spiritual" lives.[2] It is the treasure of greatest value, the one thing we cannot and will not live without.

Today, if your heart is stirred by God to see that happen, I want to close this book with a prayer that I'd encourage you to pray aloud. And may we see His Presence and power restored among us in our generation.

MY PRAYER

God, I'm making a Psalm 132 vow. I'm going to be part of building a praying church. I'm going to be a praying leader, a praying parent, a praying business professional, a praying student. I'm going to be a person of prayer.

God, remember me as I pray, see me as I pray, and stretch out Your hand, God, to do signs and wonders. Save and transform my city and the cities in my nation. Anoint the prayer meetings in my city, nation, and world.

Lord, anoint me today with the anointing to pray with vision and a prophetic spirit—to declare revival over my city, over the cities of my nation, and over this generation.

God, download the unction, the burden of Your heart, to pray and to seek Your face. Your Church needs revival. Send revival to my city and my church—start it in me.

God, for my city, anoint me to pray, to start prayer meetings. Anoint me to call people to pray to change the culture and open the heavens—to shift the heavens.

I will give no sleep to my eyes until You have a resting place here by me in my city and nation.

Remember David in all his afflictions, how he swore to You, Lord, how he vowed to the Mighty One of Jacob—"Surely, I will not go up to the comfort of my bed. I will not give sleep to my eyes or slumber to my eyelids until I find a place for the Lord."

God, I pray You would release the anointing within me that You placed within David. The anointing that laid hold of him, may it lay hold of me.

God, I pray the deepest longing of Your heart—Your zeal— would lay hold of me. Lay hold of me with Your dream, Lord, and release Your dream in the earth in the name of Jesus.

---

1. See Zechariah 10:1.
2. Brother Lawrence, *The Practice of the Presence of God* (New Kensington, PA: Whitaker House, 1982), 61.

ACKNOWLEDGMENTS

There are several people I would like to acknowledge and thank for their role in making this book come together.

It is rare to find someone who is an excellent editor that carries a prophetic mantle. Edie Mourey is just that. From the moment she heard this message taught last year at the Arise Shine Conference, she leaned in to bring that message into this book form. Edie, I can't thank you enough for being the scribe with a skillful pen as well as a lion's roar.

Krista Kennedy, my assistant and much more, I thank you for all the coordination and encouragement. Your gift of hospitality and administration is a gift to me and the people of Radiant.

Rick Burmeister, I can't thank you enough for believing in me and the vision God has entrusted me with as well as saying *yes* to leaving the marketplace in order to help me bring that vision into reality.

The people called Radiant, both in the church and the network, you are my pride and joy! I am forever grateful for the relationships that God has sent my way over the last twenty-seven years. These relationships have made me a better leader, pastor, friend, and man. I am proud of the resting place for the Lord that we have built together.

Lastly, I want to thank my wife, Jane. You are my constant and my greatest encourager. You have walked every step of this calling and journey with me, and I am forever grateful. Your sacrificial worship through every season has inspired me and given me strength. Two really are better than one. I love you with my whole heart.

ABOUT THE AUTHOR

Lee Cummings is the founding and senior leader of Radiant Church, a multi-site church reaching the globe via Radiant Church locations and online.

In addition to his role at Radiant, he is a mentor to many next-generation leaders and church planters. This role led to the launch of the Radiant Network, in which he serves as the founder and overseer.

Lee and his wife, Jane, started Radiant Church in 1996 in a high school auditorium in Richland, Michigan, a rural community in the outskirts of Kalamazoo. Since then, Radiant Church has grown to reach thousands of people in several locations with the same mission: to lead people to become radiant disciples of Jesus Christ.

Lee has authored books on Christian formation, spiritual growth, and the Spirit-empowered life. He and his wife currently reside in Kalamazoo, Michigan. They were married in 1992 and have three grown children, two sons-in-law, and three grandchildren.

You can engage with Lee via his website, https://leemcummings.com/, and the following social media sites:

- facebook.com/leemcummings
- twitter.com/leemcummings
- instagram.com/leemcummings
- youtube.com/radiantchurch
- amazon.com/author/leemcummings

ALSO BY LEE CUMMINGS

Be Radiant: Becoming Who God Meant You to Be

Flourish: Planting Your Life Where God Designed It to Thrive

School of the Spirit: Living the Holy Spirit-Empowered Life